Zentrale Prüfung

Englisch

Musteraufgaben + Test

Mittlerer Schulabschluss
Jahrgangsstufe 10 (B)
Nordrhein-Westfalen

Cornelsen

Zentrale Prüfung Englisch, Mittlerer Schulabschluss
Jahrgangsstufe 10 (B), Nordrhein-Westfalen

Erarbeitet von
David Christie, Banbury

Beratung
Wolfgang Biederstädt, Köln

Redaktion
Chris Caridia, Publishing Services, Berlin

Umschlaggestaltung
havemannundmosch, konzeption und gestaltung, Berlin

Layout und technische Umsetzung
Ingo Ostermaier

Grafik
Jeongsook Lee, Köln

Fotoquellen:
Alamy, Abington S. 8: (oben links) Mark Baigent, (oben rechts) Janine Wiedel/Photolibrary, (mitte) Janine Wiedel/Photolibrary, (unten links) Justine Kase, (unten rechts) Angie Sharp; S. 12: Angela Hampton Picture Library; S. 31 (New Zealand) Hideo Kurihara; S. 35 (eskimo in snow) Bryan & Cherry Alexander Photography, (eskimo boy) LOETSCHER CHLAUS; S. 64 (teacher) Comstock Premium, (baby) Topix
Corbis, Düsseldorf S. 43 Bettmann
Cornelsen, Berlin S. 38 (Hollywood, Grand Canyon)
Glasberg Cartoons, New York S. 62, S. 74
David Graham, London S. 10; S. 18; S. 20; S. 23; S. 30; S. 31 (Jürgen); S. 39; S. 53; S. 54 (Aisha, Rob, Kim)
iStockphoto, Canada S. 41 JBryson: S. 48 dino4; S. 49 JamesBrey; S. 51 photosmash
Picture-Alliance, Frankfurt/Main S. 38 (Elvis) Photoshot; S. 45 dpa
Shutterstock, New York S. 54 (Ashley, Mariah)

Textquellen
p14 The Project (from *I told you*, adapted with permission): Suvi Mahonen, Australia 2009
p58 An experiment (from *A Most Ambitious Experiment*, adapted with permission): Mike Krath, USA 2009

www.cornelsen.de

1. Auflage, 1. Druck 2009

Druck: CS-Druck CornelsenStürtz, Berlin

ISBN 978-3-06-032287-9

Inhalt gedruckt auf säurefreiem Papier aus nachhaltiger Forstwirtschaft.

INHALT

Liebe Schülerin, lieber Schüler!

Dieses Heft soll dir helfen, dich auf die zentrale Prüfung am Ende der Klasse 10 vorzubereiten. Es enthält unterschiedliche Beispiele für Testaufgaben, wie sie dir so oder ähnlich auch in der Prüfung begegnen werden. Wenn du diese Übungen durcharbeitest, kannst du zuversichtlich sein, dass du weißt, was in der zentralen Prüfung am Ende der Klasse 10 auf dich zukommt, und dass du die unterschiedlichen Aufgabenstellungen geübt hast.

Was beinhaltet die zentrale Prüfung am Ende der Klasse 10?

Der Schwerpunkt der zentralen Prüfung am Ende der Klasse 10 kann sich von Jahr zu Jahr unterscheiden: Entweder liegt er auf der Lese- und Schreibkompetenz oder aber auf der Hör- und Schreibkompetenz in der englischen Sprache. Als weiterer Prüfungsschwerpunkt kann ggf. auch ein Sprechfertigkeitstest hinzukommen. Deine Lehrerin oder dein Lehrer wird dir mitteilen, welche Art von Test du ablegen musst.

Der schriftliche Test hat zwei Teile, unabhängig davon, ob er aus Lesen und Schreiben oder aus Hören und Schreiben besteht. In Teil 1 geht es um die Überprüfung deines Hör- oder Leseverstehens. Ausgangspunkt hierzu ist ein Lesetext oder eine Tonaufnahme, zu dem oder der du Verständnisfragen beantworten musst. Teil 2 des Tests ist anspruchsvoller. Er geht ebenfalls von einem Text aus, prüft aber zunächst deine Vokabelkenntnisse und endet mit einigen Schreibaufgaben.

Ein sehr wichtiger Punkt, den du im Hinterkopf behalten solltest, wenn du mit diesem Heft arbeitest, ist, dass Teil 2 des Tests schulformspezifisch ist. Er unterscheidet sich also leicht für die Schüler/innen an unterschiedlichen Schulformen. Hauptzielgruppen sind:
(1) Schüler/innen der Hauptschule (Typ 10 B) bzw. der Erweiterungskurse an Gesamtschulen und Realschulen;
(2) Gymnasialschüler/innen. In diesem Heft werden diese beiden Gruppen als **A** und **B** bezeichnet. Der Aufbau der Testaufgaben ist daher wie folgt organisiert:

Teil 1	Teil 2
Hörverstehen bzw. Leseverstehen für alle Schüler/innen	**2 A Leseverstehen – Wortschatz – Schreiben** HS Typ 10B, Ges EK, RS
	2 B Vom Ausgangstext zum Zieltext Gymnasium

Natürlich kannst du auch versuchen, die Übungen zu machen, die nicht speziell für deine Gruppe vorgesehen sind. Dies übt zusätzlich[1].

Teil 1 des Tests

Der erste Teil des Tests, der für alle Schüler/innen gleich ist, besteht aus einem Hörtext (oder Lesetext). Dazu musst du Fragen beantworten und zeigen, dass du die Hauptaussagen des Textes verstanden hast. Wenn der Text ein Hörtext ist, wirst du ihn zweimal hören. Die Fragen können unterschiedlich formuliert sein. Die Hauptkategorien von Verständnisfragen sind:

- *multiple choice:* Hier werden dir 3–4 mögliche Antworten zu einer Frage angeboten und du musst die richtige Antwort heraussuchen, indem du das richtige Kästchen ankreuzt.
- *true/false:* Bei derartigen Aufgaben musst du entscheiden, ob die vorgegebene Aussage über den Text wahr oder falsch ist. – Manchmal gibt es sogar noch eine dritte Kategorie (*true, false or no information in the text*), für den Fall, dass dir der Text keine Auskunft darüber gibt, ob die Aussage wahr oder falsch ist, weil er diese spezielle Information nicht enthält.
- *write-in answers:* Hier musst du eine Frage kurz schriftlich beantworten, ein fehlendes Wort einfügen oder einen Satz ergänzen.
- *matching:* Bei diesen Aufgaben musst du z. B. Textstellen Bildern oder bestimmte Aussagen Personen zuordnen.

1 *In der Prüfung musst du dich nicht zwischen einer A- und B-Version entscheiden. Deine Prüfungsunterlagen beinhalten nur Aufgaben, die für dich vorgesehen sind.*

Teil 2 des Tests

• 2 A Leseverstehen – Wortschatz – Schreiben (für Hauptschule Typ 10 B, Gesamtschule EK und Realschule)

Wenn du ein/e Schüler/in an einer der oben genannten Schulformen bist, solltest du jetzt zu Teil 2 A in diesem Heft weiterblättern. Aufgabe 1 ist ein Lesetext. Er kann u. U. etwas länger sein als der Text in Teil 1. Der wichtigste Unterschied ist aber, dass das in diesem Text eingeführte Thema dich durch den gesamten Rest der Prüfungsaufgaben begleiten wird.

Es können Fragen wie in Teil 1 gestellt werden. Die zweite Aufgabe in Teil 2 testet speziell deine Wortschatzkenntnis. Unterschiedliche Aufgaben sind möglich, vom multiple choice bis hin zum Lückentext. Eine Art von Aufgaben, die du antreffen wirst, ist das mindmapping. Eine typische Aufgabenstellung könnte dich auffordern, mehr Wörter zu finden (Find more words ...), um sie einer Mindmap hinzuzufügen. Der zu ergänzende Wortschatz stammt meist aus dem Themenbereich, der sich durch den ganzen 2. Teil der Prüfung zieht. Wenn das Thema also zum Beispiel holidays ist, dann könnte die Vokabelaufgabe nach Wörtern und Formulierungen fragen, die mit Reisen, Ferienzielen oder der Beschreibung von Reiseeindrücken oder Orten zu tun haben.

Die abschließende dritte Aufgabe in Teil 2 besteht aus drei Schreibaufgaben. Es kann sein, dass du aufgefordert wirst, den Ausgangstext von Teil 2 zusammenzufassen, deine eigene Meinung über das Thema zu äußern oder vielleicht auch einen Brief oder eine E-Mail zu verfassen. Dabei wird beabsichtigt, dass du Wörter und Formulierungen, die du in der Wortschatzaufgabe gesammelt hast, nun als Hilfe zum Schreiben der verlangten Textsorte verwendest.

• 2 B Vom Ausgangstext zum Zieltext (Gymnasium)

Wenn du ein/e Schüler/in am Gymnasium bist, kannst du jetzt bei Teil 2 B dieses Hefts weitermachen. Dieser Teil der Prüfung verbindet Leseverstehen und Textaufgaben in einem Prozess, in dem du aus einem Ausgangstext einen Zieltext erarbeiten musst. Im Wesentlichen läuft dies folgendermaßen ab: Du erhältst einen Lesetext, der in ein Thema einführt. Es gibt keine Fragen direkt zum Text wie in Teil 1. Stattdessen gibt es:

(1) Wortschatzübungen, die zwei Ziele haben: zum einen soll deine allgemeine Wortschatzkenntnis zum Themenbereich dieses Prüfungsteils getestet werden, zum anderen hilft sie dir, Wörter und Formulierungen für die folgende Aufgaben zu sammeln.

(2) Schreibaufgaben: In der Regel werden drei Aufgaben gestellt. Du sollst in zusammenhängenden Texten beschreiben, erzählen, berichten, zusammenfassen und/oder argumentieren.

Welche Themen und Texte werden in der Prüfung vorkommen?

Wichtiger Hinweis: In der Prüfung wird nicht dein Wissen über ein Thema oder ein Land abgefragt. Das Themenfeld dient nur als Rahmen für den Test. Die Fragen zielen nur auf die Sprache und den Inhalt der einzelnen Texte ab. Du musst in der Prüfungsvorbereitung daher keine Zeit aufwenden, etwas über diese Themenfelder zu lernen.

Die Texte in der Prüfung beziehen sich auf alle englischsprachigen Länder (Großbritannien, Australien, Kanada etc.), aber der Großteil wird die USA betreffen.

Lesetexte können Artikel aus Zeitungen oder Zeitschriften, Briefe und E-Mails, Weblogs und andere Texte von Internetseiten, Informationsbroschüren, Gedichte oder Liedtexte sein. Für Schüler/innen vom Gymnasium können aber durchaus auch Kurzgeschichten oder Auszüge aus Romanen ausgewählt werden. Hörtexte können entweder von einer Person gesprochen (Monologe) oder Unterhaltungen zwischen zwei oder mehr Personen sein. Aber auch Interviews oder kurze Radiosendungen können präsentiert werden. Alle Textsorten, denen du in der Prüfung begegnest, werden dir aus deinem Englischunterricht vertraut sein.

VORSCHLÄGE, UM BESSERE NOTEN IN DER PRÜFUNG ZU ERZIELEN

- Zeiteinteilung ist wichtig. Besonders im Teil 2 der Prüfung ist es notwendig, dass du deine Zeit für die Antworten sorgfältig planst. Dieser Teil besteht aus mehreren unterschiedlichen Aufgaben, für die du jeweils Zeit einplanen solltest. Plane am Ende mindestens fünf Minuten ein, um deine Antworten noch einmal durchzugehen. Stelle sicher, dass du eine Uhr zur Prüfung mitnimmst und behalte die Zeit im Auge. Wenn du feststellst, dass du dich an einer der Fragen zu lange aufhältst, ist es besser, erstmal mit der nächsten Frage weiterzumachen und gegebenenfalls am Ende noch einmal auf sie zurückzukommen.
- Lies die Aufgabenstellung sehr gründlich durch und beantworte die Fragen. Das klingt zunächst leicht, ist es aber nicht. Hat nicht jeder schon einmal Punkte in einer Klassenarbeit abgezogen bekommen, weil er die Aufgabenstellung verfehlt hat? Nimm dir Zeit und lies die Fragestellung genau durch. Achte beim Schreiben darauf, dass du auf alle Punkte der Fragestellung eingehst.
- Die Fähigkeit, Texte zu lesen (oder zu hören) und zu verstehen, ist sicherlich im Englischunterricht geübt worden. Denk daran, niemand erwartet von dir, dass du jedes einzelne Wort verstehst. Es wird immer Wörter geben, über deren Bedeutung du dir nicht sicher bist oder ganze Sätze, die dir nicht hundertprozentig klar sind. Entscheidend ist, dass du zunächst im Großen und Ganzen verstehst, wovon der Text handelt. Wenn du so weit bist, können einzelne Teile des Texts geklärt und deren Bedeutung erschlossen werden. Lesetexte solltest du mehrmals durchlesen. Hörübungen wirst du immer zweimal hören.
- Unterschiedliche Textsorten zu schreiben, ist ein wichtiger Teil der Prüfung. Je mehr Übung du im Schreiben von speziellen Textsorten bekommen kannst, desto besser. Genau hierfür bietet dir dieses Heft genug Möglichkeiten. Es wird dir helfen, die folgenden Hinweise zu beachten:
  (1) Plane, was du sagen willst (denk daran, auf alle Punkte, die die Frage fordert, auch wirklich einzugehen). Wenn du keine genaue Vorstellung hast, bevor du anfängst zu schreiben, wird dir das Schreiben sehr viel schwerer fallen.
  (2) Formuliere klare Sätze. Vermeide es, komplizierte deutsche Sätze wörtwörtlich ins Englische übersetzen zu wollen. Vergiss nicht, deine Wörter zu zählen. Die Aufgaben verlangen immer eine Mindestwortzahl (zum Beispiel 100 Wörter). Achte darauf, dass du nicht viel mehr und nicht viel weniger schreibst.
  (3) Kontrolliere am Ende, was du geschrieben hast. Einzelne Fehler findest du immer.
  Versuche, ruhig zu bleiben und dich auf die Aufgaben zu konzentrieren. Auf den ersten Blick sieht ein Test immer schwierig aus! Schau dir den ganzen Test zuerst in Ruhe an und versuche, einen Eindruck von den Aufgabenstellungen zu bekommen. Dann gehe zurück an den Anfang und beginne, sorgfältig (Schritt für Schritt) zu arbeiten. Du wirst merken, dass das, was am Anfang schwierig aussah, schnell zu einer Folge von Aufgaben wird, die du bewältigen kannst.

Wir wünschen dir viel Erfolg für deine Prüfung!

Teil I

Hörverstehen

Test one

Detailliertes Verstehen

1.1 My first day at work

You are going to hear a young British woman, Becky, talking about her first day at work.

First read the tasks below. You have 90 seconds to do this. Then listen to the dialogue and tick the correct box or complete the sentence. You will hear the story ***twice****.*

Useful vocabulary

to apply for a job *sich um eine Stelle bewerben*
company *Unternehmen, Firma*
piece of advice *Ratschlag*
receptionist *Empfangsmitarbeiter/in*

1 After Becky left school, she trained for a year as a

a) ☐ nurse.

b) ☐ shop assistant.

c) ☐ secretary.

2 After that, she got a job in a nice company in

____

______________________________.

3 The piece of advice everyone gave Becky about her first day at work was

a) ☐ "Don't be late on your first day!"

b) ☐ "Wear smart clothes!"

c) ☐ "Don't expect to know everything straight away."

4 Becky woke up on Monday, September 1st at

a) ☐ 6 o'clock.

b) ☐ 9 o'clock.

c) ☐ 8.25.

5 She says she threw on some clothes, washed her face, ____________________

____________________, and ran out of the house.

6 When Becky got outside in the street, her bus

a) ☐ was standing at the bus stop.

b) ☐ was just coming.

c) ☐ had just left.

7 She started to cross the street and a ____________________

____________________.

8 Becky shouted something which included the word '____________________'.

9 When Becky arrived at work she felt

a) ☐ really stressed out.

b) ☐ calm.

c) ☐ nervous.

10 The first person she met was

a) ☐ the receptionist at the reception desk.

b) ☐ her new boss.

c) ☐ the woman who had interviewed her for the job.

11 What happened when Becky went into Mr Murray's office? Write one or two short sentences to explain.

____

____

12 Which of these statements best summarises Becky's story?

a) ☐ Her job started badly and got worse.

b) ☐ Her job started well and got better.

c) ☐ Her job started badly but got better.

Selektives Verstehen

1.2 Announcements and messages

You are going to hear five short texts.

First read the statements below. You have 60 seconds to do this. Then listen to the texts and decide whether the statements are true or false. You will hear each text ***twice****.*
Mark your answers while you are listening.

1

You are travelling by train from New York Central Station to Boston. You have just left Central Station when the train stops, and you hear the following announcement: ...

You will be unable to travel to Boston today. true ☐ false ☐

2

You are going to hear an answerphone message for Chrissy's mom. This is what Chrissy says: ...

Chrissy is not coming home tonight. true ☐ false ☐

3

You are in London. You are listening to the radio when the weather forecast comes on. ...

It's going to rain in the Midlands and Wales. true ☐ false ☐

4

You are in a supermarket in Sydney when you hear the following announcement: ...

Frozen foods are cheaper all this week. true ☐ false ☐

5

You are in an aeroplane travelling from London to Berlin when you hear the following announcement: ...

German time is not the same as British time. true ☐ false ☐

Globales Verstehen

1.3 Healthy eating

You are going to hear five people talking about their eating habits.

First read the statements below. Listen to the people and choose the correct statement for each person. Write the correct letters in the spaces while you are listening. After that you will hear the people again. There is one statement that you don't need.

A Everyone can learn to cook.

B It is not difficult to have a healthy diet.

C Healthy food is boring.

D There is too much advertising for unhealthy food.

E Everyone knows which foods are unhealthy.

F Special labels would help people to know which foods are healthy.

Person	Statement
Liza	
Nadja	
Daniel	
Adam	
Ashley	

Test two

Detailliertes Verstehen

2.1 My plans for the future

You are going to hear two teenagers from different parts of the world talking about their plans for the future.

First read the tasks below. You have 90 seconds to do this. Then listen to the dialogue and tick the correct box. You will hear both teenagers ***twice****.*

1 Matt's favourite subjects at school are

a) ☐ sport and history.

b) ☐ math and history.

c) ☐ music and sport.

2 Which hobbies does Matt **not** mention?

a) ☐ water sports such as surfing.

b) ☐ playing the guitar in a band.

c) ☐ playing baseball and volleyball at school.

3 How many more years does Matt plan to stay in high school?

a) ☐ two

b) ☐ one

c) ☐ four

4 What does Matt say about his future job?

a) ☐ He doesn't want to work with people all the time.

b) ☐ He knows exactly what he wants to do.

c) ☐ He thinks he would like marketing.

5 Like all teenagers, Zoe

a) ☐ likes photography and painting.

b) ☐ listens to music and goes out with friends.

c) ☐ wants to go to university.

6 Which of these statements is true?

a) ☐ Zoe loves all her school subjects.

b) ☐ Zoe has to travel a long way to go swimming.

c) ☐ Zoe wants to study in Sydney.

7 When did Zoe decide that she would like to become an architect?

a) ☐ When she was a child.

b) ☐ When she was at high school.

c) ☐ When she moved to Sydney.

8 Zoe thinks being an architect would be a good job for her because

a) ☐ she lives in a big city.

b) ☐ she is a very active person.

c) ☐ she loves art.

Selektives Verstehen

2.2 My year abroad

Jürgen Zeller from Germany is spending a year at a high school in New Zealand. You are going to hear him talking about his experiences there.

First read about the high school on this page from its website.

GERALDINE HIGH SCHOOL

About us

Geraldine High School is a mixed school of 520 students from ages 11–18. It is situated in the small township of Geraldine on New Zealand's South Island.

The school is one of New Zealand's most successful schools academically. Our students also take part in many cultural and outdoor sporting activities, from skiing to rock climbing and kayaking to rafting.

Each year we welcome a number of international students. During their year with us, the students live in carefully-chosen host families in the safe and friendly township of Geraldine. In school, we offer international students lessons in English as a Second Language (ESL). We also advise them to study a smaller number of subjects than at home, so that they can make full use of their year in New Zealand.

*First read the statements below. You have 60 seconds to do this. Then listen and decide whether the statements are true or false. You will hear the text **twice**. Mark your answers while you are listening.*

		true	false
1	Jürgen arrived in New Zealand four months ago.	☐	☐
2	Geraldine High School is a long way from where Jürgen is staying.	☐	☐
3	Jürgen goes to school alone.	☐	☐
4	When Jürgen left Germany it was summer.	☐	☐
5	It is too cold for outdoor activities in winter in New Zealand.	☐	☐
6	In New Zealand Jürgen is doing fewer than half the number of subjects he had to do in Germany.	☐	☐
7	There are seven other international students apart from Jürgen.	☐	☐
8	Some pupils have organized trips for Jürgen to cities such as Christchurch and Wellington.	☐	☐
9	There are lots of good shops in Geraldine.	☐	☐
10	The main reason Jürgen went to New Zealand was to improve his English.	☐	☐

Globales Verstehen

2.3 Computers

You are going to hear five people talking about computers.

First read the statements below. Listen to the people and choose the correct statement for each person. Write the correct letters in the spaces while you are listening. After that you will hear the five people again. There is one statement that you don't need.

A Computers can stop people making real social contacts.

B People who spend too much time at the computer get health problems.

C Time spent at the computer is not always wasted time.

D There is a danger of becoming addicted to the computer if you don't learn to deal with it in a sensible way.

E The government thinks internet addicts need to go to a special place.

F There are more important things to do than play computer games.

Person	Statement
Linda	
Craig	
Jacqui	
Scott	
Robert	

TEST THREE

Detailliertes Verstehen

3.1 What's your favourite movie?

Listen and answer the questions below. You will hear the friends' conversation ***twice****.*

1 Beth's favourite movie is Titanic because she likes
- a) ☐ action movies.
- b) ☐ romantic movies.
- c) ☐ comedies.
- d) ☐ historical movies.

2 When Beth saw Titanic she
- a) ☐ fell in love with Leonardo DiCaprio.
- b) ☐ cried when she came out of the cinema.
- c) ☐ stayed in the cinema and watched the film a second time.
- d) ☐ bought a big poster of the movie.

3 Amber thought Titanic was
- a) ☐ awesome[1].
- b) ☐ too sad.
- c) ☐ boring.
- d) ☐ too long.

1 ***awesome (American English)*** *stark, toll*

4 She tells the others about a movie with the title
- a) ☐ Jack Black.
- b) ☐ The Rock Band.
- c) ☐ Cool Kids.
- d) ☐ School of Rock.

Jon (the boy on the right), Beth (the girl on the left) and Amber are American high school friends. They're talking about their favourite movies.

5 At the end of this movie some young kids win ______________________________.

6 Jon's favourite movie is ______________________________.

7 He thinks the best thing about this movie is the

a) ☐ director.

b) ☐ special effects.

c) ☐ costumes.

d) ☐ music.

8 Beth remembers that the director of this movie

a) ☐ wrote all the films himself.

b) ☐ acted in two of the movies.

c) ☐ was also the cameraman.

d) ☐ invented some new computer techniques.

9 At the end, the friends have to finish their conversation because ______________________________

______________________________.

Selektives Verstehen

3.2 Writing and reading books

You are going to hear a radio programme from the USA. The programme is an interview with a young American writer, Christopher Primo.

First read the statements below. You have 60 seconds to do this. Then listen and decide whether the statements are true or false. You will hear the interview twice. Mark your answers while you are listening.

		true	false
1	Christopher's education was unusual.	☐	☐
2	Christopher got his high school diploma four years ago.	☐	☐
3	Christopher has no brothers or sisters.	☐	☐
4	It took three years to write the whole trilogy.	☐	☐
5	When Christopher wrote *Dragonland*, he was already an experienced writer.	☐	☐
6	Christopher likes reading fantasy stories.	☐	☐
7	All the characters in *Dragonland* are out of Christopher's head.	☐	☐
8	Christopher lives in a place like Dragonland.	☐	☐
9	Christopher thinks it is important to plan a story carefully.	☐	☐
10	You can buy two of the three books.	☐	☐

Globales Verstehen

3.3 Coming to America

You are going to hear four people talking about immigrating to the United States.

First read the statements below. Listen to the radio programme and choose the correct statements. There are two statements for each person. Write the correct letters in the spaces while you are listening. You will hear the programme ***twice****.*

A There are some things I miss from my home country.

B There were ten of us living in two rooms.

C I saw thousands of people in the Immigration Building.

D People were interested in me because I was from another country.

E My brother and sister were too old to come with us.

F We were worried they wouldn't let us in.

G We were shocked at how dirty everything was.

H My mom is not completely happy here.

Person	Statement
Larry	
Maria	
Miriam	
Fali	

Larry

Maria

TEST FOUR

Detailliertes Verstehen

4.1 Horrible jobs

You are going to hear three people, Peter, Jill and Adil, talking about horrible jobs.

First read the tasks below. You have 90 seconds to do this. Then listen to the conversation and tick the correct box or complete the sentence. You will hear the discussion ***twice****.*

Useful vocabulary

woodcutter *Holzfäller*
death rate *Sterberate*
disgusting *ekelhaft*
watchman *Wächter*

1 The worst kind of job Peter can imagine is

a) ☐ a boring job.
b) ☐ a dangerous job.
c) ☐ a dirty job.

2 The three most dangerous jobs in America are woodcutter,

____

and __________________________.

3 Adil wonders

a) ☐ who makes burgers for a living.
b) ☐ who kills animals for a living.
c) ☐ who makes chicken soup for a living.

4 Which one of the speakers doesn't eat meat?

a) ☐ Adil
b) ☐ Jill
c) ☐ Peter

5 Adil talks about dirty jobs such as working in a ______________________________.

6 Peter talks about a factory that produces

a) ☐ blue cheese dip.
b) ☐ chicken wings.
c) ☐ burgers.

7 Peter heard about the factory

a) ☐ on the radio.

b) ☐ in the newspaper.

c) ☐ on TV.

8 What did Adil find disgusting about his job in the restaurant kitchen?

a) ☐ The low pay.

b) ☐ The bin of leftover food.

c) ☐ The accident he had with the knives and forks.

9 Peter found his job as nightwatchman boring because he had

____ and ____.

10 Jill found her telephone job frustrating because

a) ☐ people didn't answer the phone.

b) ☐ she often got the wrong number.

c) ☐ people hung up on her.

Selektives Verstehen

4.2 Brothers and sisters

You are going to hear three teenagers talking about their brothers and sisters.

First read the statements below. You have 60 seconds to do this. Then listen and decide whether the statements are true or false. You will hear the discussion ***twice****. Mark your answers while you are listening.*

		true	false
1	Tansu sometimes wants to do things her brothers don't want her to do.	☐	☐
2	Chloe doesn't have any brothers.	☐	☐
3	Chloe's sister was really upset when Chloe cut off her hair.	☐	☐
4	Both Chloe's parents were angry with her.	☐	☐
5	Jamie often visits his sister.	☐	☐
6	Jamie's sister is training to be a teacher.	☐	☐
7	Jamie doesn't have much in common with his brother.	☐	☐
8	Chloe thinks things are easier for her sister.	☐	☐
9	Tansu thinks being the youngest has no disadvantages.	☐	☐
10	Chloe wishes she was on only child.	☐	☐

Globales Verstehen

4.3 Emotions

You are going to hear five people talking about emotions.

First read the statements below. Listen to the people and choose the correct statement for each person. Write the correct letters in the spaces while you are listening. After that you will hear the five people again. There is one statement that you don't need.

A Sport can help you to deal with your anger.

B Crying is healthy.

C 'Road rage' is when drivers get angry and aggressive.

D Crying and laughing are equally important.

E People in the country show their emotions more than people in the city.

F Showing anger and aggression is often a way of hiding other emotions.

Person	Statement
Rebecca	
Emmie	
Daniel	
Ryan	
Adam	

TEST FIVE

Detailliertes Verstehen

5.1 Horror movies

You are going to hear three people talking about horror movies.

First read the tasks below. You have 90 seconds to do this. Then listen to the dialogue and tick the correct box. You will hear all three speakers ***twice****.*

Useful vocabulary

coffin *Sarg*
custodian *Aufsichtsperson*
haunt *spuken,* ***the place is haunted*** *dort spukt es*
drive somebody mad *jemanden verrückt machen*

1 Which of the following statements about *Psycho* is **not** true?

a) ☐ It stars Alfred Hitchcock.
b) ☐ It is one of the most frightening movies of all times.
c) ☐ It is a black and white film.

2 Why does Marion stop at Bates Motel?

a) ☐ Because it is on the highway.
b) ☐ Because it is managed by a nice, quiet guy.
c) ☐ Because there is a terrible storm.

3 Who murdered Marion?

a) ☐ Mrs Bates
b) ☐ Norman Bates
c) ☐ Anthony Perkins

4 Which of the following statements about *The Vanishing* is true?

a) ☐ Nobody knows what happened to Diane.
b) ☐ The last scene is the most frightening.
c) ☐ Most of the story is about Barney's family.

5 Where did Jeff last see Diane?

a) ☐ At a picnic.
b) ☐ In a coffin.
c) ☐ At a gas station.

6 In the last scene of the film, Jeff

a) ☐ is in danger of his life.

b) ☐ finds Diana's coffin.

c) ☐ escapes.

7 The speaker says that Jack Torrance is one of Jack Nicholson's ...

a) ☐ favourite roles.

b) ☐ best roles.

c) ☐ most frightening roles.

8 Jack's job at the Overlook Hotel is

a) ☐ to help the hotel guests.

b) ☐ to take care of the hotel while it is closed.

c) ☐ to write a novel about the hotel.

9 The "shining" is

a) ☐ the ability to haunt places.

b) ☐ the thing that drives Jack mad.

c) ☐ the power to see things in the past and future.

10 Danny is afraid

a) ☐ that his father might murder him and his mother.

b) ☐ that Mr Grady's ghost will kill his family.

c) ☐ because the hotel is haunted.

Selektives Verstehen

5.2 Nightmares

You are going to hear three people talking about nightmares.

First read the statements below. You have 60 seconds to do this. Then listen and decide whether the statements are true or false. You will hear the discussion ***twice****. Mark your answers while you are listening.*

		true	false
1	Ryan is tired because he went to bed late.	☐	☐
2	Ryan dreamed that he lost his parents.	☐	☐
3	Ryan always has nightmares when he watches horror movies.	☐	☐
4	A long time ago Lucy had a nightmare about spiders.	☐	☐
5	Lucy sometimes has nightmares when she has been to the cinema.	☐	☐
6	Jake dreamt about being bitten by a big dog.	☐	☐
7	Lucy has sometimes had the same kind of dreams as Jake.	☐	☐
8	Jake heard something interesting about nightmares on the radio.	☐	☐
9	Nightmares are always a result of stress.	☐	☐
10	Having nightmares is not normal.	☐	☐

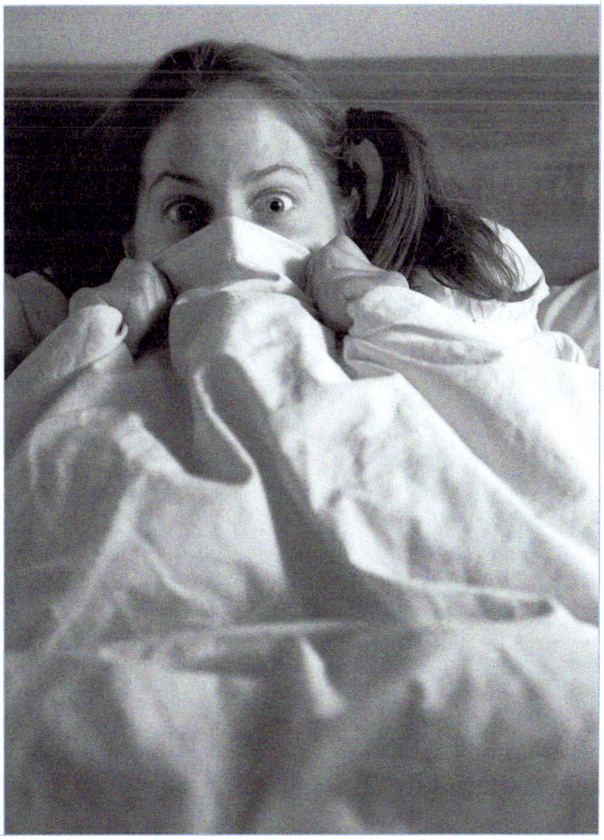

Globales Verstehen

5.3 Friendship

You are going to hear five people talking about friendship.

First read the statements below. Listen to the people and choose the correct statement for each person. Write the correct letters in the spaces while you are listening. After that you will hear the five people again. There is one statement that you don't need.

A A good friend always has time for you.

B Don't be envious[1] of your friends.

C In a real friendship there should be no "boss" who decides everything.

D It's important to keep your promises.

E Forgive mistakes. We all make them.

F Be honest with your friends.

1 ***envious*** *neidisch*

Person	Statement
Finlay	
Sophie	
Conor	
Harry	
Isabelle	

Leseverstehen

Test one

1.1 Who speaks English?

The following text deals with English as a world language and introduces some people from around the world who speak English.

First read the whole text. Then read the tasks.
Read the text again and do the tasks. Tick the correct box or write down the correct answer.

Roughly 1.5 billion people around the world today speak English. By 2015, experts say that English will be spoken by three billion people – almost half the world's population. But what does 'speak English' mean? Let's look at some different people who use English every day.

Native speakers

Kathy

Marty

Alison

Kathy from Britain, Marty from the USA, and Alison from Australia are all native speakers of English. That means English is the first language of their country and it is the language that they all speak every day. There are few other countries where English is also the first language: New Zealand is an example. Altogether, there are around 360 million native speakers of English around the world. By far the most live in the USA.

English as an official language

Yvonne

Yvonne from East Africa and Vinesh from India live in countries where English is an official language. They speak it at school, often read newspapers in English, and if they travelled to Britain or the USA, they would be able to speak English easily. English is still their second language, however, and it is only an official language for them because they live in countries which were once British colonies. Yvonne's first language is Swahili and Vinesh's is Hindi.

Vinesh

English – the global language

Anischa

Chi Hieu

Anischa, a 10th grade student from Germany, and Chi Hieu from Vietnam also speak English, and for them it is also a second language, one which they are learning at school. So what do these two teenagers from very different places have in common? The answer is simple: for Anischa and Chi Hieu, English is the language of much pop culture, the internet and above all of business. Around the world, English is now the global language and if you can't speak it, then you can't enter the 'global village' of today's world. Anischa will certainly need English for her job later in life. For Chi Hieu in Vietnam, the language is perhaps even more important. For him – and for other young Vietnamese – speaking English means being able to travel and to trade worldwide.

1 Which statement below best summarises the ideas in the text?

a) ☐ Everyone in the world should speak English.

b) ☐ One day everyone in the world will speak English.

c) ☐ Only native speakers speak English well.

d) ☐ English is the language people worldwide use to communicate.

2 How many people around the world are native speakers of English?

a) ☐ 1.5 billion

b) ☐ 360 million

c) ☐ 3 billion

d) ☐ nearly half the world's population

3 Name four countries where people are native speakers of English.

a) ______________________________

b) ______________________________

c) ______________________________

d) ______________________________

4 Why do people in East Africa speak English?

a) ☐ Because it is a global language.

b) ☐ Because all newspapers in their country are in English.

c) ☐ Because the British once had a colony in their country.

d) ☐ Because they want to travel to Britain one day.

5 Where are Anischa from Germany and Chi Hieu from Vietnam learning English?

____

____

6 According to the text, why is it important for Anischa and Chi Hieu to speak English?

a) ☐ Because they want to use the Internet.

b) ☐ Because if they can't speak English, they won't be able to enter the "global village" later in their lives.

c) ☐ Because English is their favourite subject at school.

d) ☐ Because they both speak English as a second language.

7 What is English the global language for? Give three examples from the text.

a) ______________________________

b) ______________________________

c) ______________________________

8 Why is it particularly important for people in Chi Hieu's country to speak English?

a) ☐ They need the language so they can go to school.

b) ☐ They need English to travel to and do business with other countries worldwide.

c) ☐ They won't get a job if they can't speak English.

d) ☐ They won't understand pop culture if they don't know English.

1.2 Looking for a job

Six young people are looking for jobs. The adverts below are from a local newspaper.

First read the statements about the people (0 – 5) and then read the job adverts (A – G). Decide which job would be best for each person. Write the correct letters in the grid below. There are more job adverts than people.

0	1	2	3	4	5
G					

0 Sandra

"Remember Knut, the polar bear in the Berlin Zoo? He was so cute. I'd love to have a job working with animals like that. I've always had animals to look after at home ever since I was a little kid."

1 Aisha

"I think I'm a friendly person. I like meeting new people. At school, my favourite subjects are art and music. At home my mum and dad have a beautiful garden. I love helping my dad when he works there."

2 Rob

"I have lots of hobbies. I like sport, computers, music and reading. I have a lot of friends, and they say that I'm a friendly person. I'd like a job where I meet lots of people, but not in an office or a shop. At school my favourite subjects are German and maths."

3 Kim

"I definitely don't want to work in an office! I like being outside. I think I'm also a very practical person. I like doing things with my hands. When I was a kid, I always made things – toys, a little house in the garden. I have a car driving licence."

4 Ashley

"I like being on my own and I don't really want to work with other people. I really enjoy driving. and travelling. I have a motorbike licence and a car licence and as soon as I'm 21, I want to get a category C licence, so that I can drive bigger vehicles."

5 Mariah

"I enjoy working with computers and I can type really fast. My friends say that I have a pleasant voice on the telephone. I've often helped my dad in his office during the school holidays, and I enjoyed it."

JOBS

A

AUTOCAR

Our Autocar workshop in Watford is looking for qualified car mechanics.

Good pay and conditions.

Interested?

Call 0751-554321
between 7.30 a.m. and 5.30 p.m.

B

The Manor Hotel

is looking for a
Receptionist

We need a receptionist to meet hotel guests, answer the phone, and book rooms. We will give you training for the job. French or German an advantage.
Contact:
Mary Summerfield on:
01865 711548
between 9 a.m. and 2 p.m.

C

MIDLAND BUILDERS

We have two apprenticeships for

CARPENTERS

in our building firm.
Apprentices work three days in the firm and have two days free for study at a college.

If you are interested, ring:
01221–211347

D

WANTED

Lorry drivers

Must have experience and a full HGV driving licence.

For more information contact

Paul Roberts on 01549–301299

E

Dawn's Flowers

We are looking for someone to work in our small, friendly flower shop in the town centre.

If you are good with people and love plants and flowers, please come in and see us!

F

SECRETARY WANTED
FOR OUR BUSY OFFICE

We are looking for a person to type letters, answer the phone and do general office work in our busy town centre office.

Experience of computers would be good.

Write to: P.O. Box[3] 117.

G

Wilsford Zoo

is looking for apprentice animal keepers.

If you are over 16, love animals and would like to train with us,

phone us now on 0742-55673

Test two

2.1 Are you addicted to the internet?

The following text is an article from a magazine for European teenagers.

First read the whole text. Then read the tasks.
Read the text again and do the tasks. Tick the correct box or write down the correct answer.

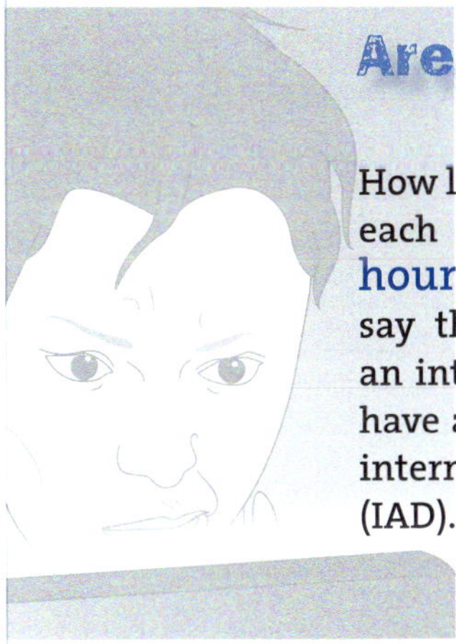

Are you addicted to the internet?

How long do you spend online each day? An hour? Two hours? More? Psychologists say that it is possible to be an internet addict. They even have a name for the problem: internet Addiction Disorder[1] (IAD).

All over the world, teenagers of the web generation are spending more and more time online. The internet can be a wonderful thing, of course. You can chat to friends, get help with homework, send and receive emails and much more.

But for a few people, surfing the web is more than just a pleasant or useful thing to do. These are the people who are suffering[2] from IAD. They spend many hours alone in front of their computer 'speaking' only to people sometimes thousands of miles away. This means that they often don't have normal friendships. Sitting for so long in front of the computer also means that they get no exercise, and often they don't eat properly – they have snacks at their desk rather than regular, healthy meals. The biggest problem seems to be with people who play online games – some spend up to 17 hours a day during holidays just doing this!

We all use the internet nowadays, so just because you go online – even if you use the internet a lot – it doesn't mean that you're an addict! Remember that people with IAD are an extreme case! It's like everything in life: there are lots of good things, but sometimes you can have too much of one thing. When that changes your life, then that's when you can start having problems.

Did you know?

In Germany there's a special four-week summer camp for internet addicts. People can only go online half an hour a day and have to play lots of sports.

What you've told us ...

I love going on the internet, but I also love reading, going shopping with friends etc, so I don't think I'm addicted.
Emily, 16, England

I definitely couldn't live without my computer. I spend all my time on it.
Anton, 17, The Netherlands

I love spending time online, but I'm not an addict! Perhaps some people are, but I think the camp in Germany is stupid!
Jens, 16, Germany

I think the internet is the greatest invention ever. How could I chat to all my English friends without it?
Sophie, 15, France

1 ***disorder*** *Störung, Krankheit*
2 ***to suffer from (an illnes)*** *an (einer Krankheit) leiden*

1 According to the article, how many of all the young people who use the internet are addicted to it?

a) ☐ Everyone.

b) ☐ Most of them.

c) ☐ About 17 per cent.

d) ☐ Only a small number.

2 People who have IAD

a) ☐ have normal conversations with people all over the world.

b) ☐ have regular healthy meals at their desks.

c) ☐ live unhealthy lives.

d) ☐ have problems with people who play online games.

3 The article says

a) ☐ it's not good to do any one thing too much.

b) ☐ we should do good things as often as we want.

c) ☐ using a computer is not a good thing.

d) ☐ The internet is harmless.

4 There is a special camp in Germany where internet addicts

a) ☐ can spend all day at the computer.

b) ☐ are not allowed to use the computer at all.

c) ☐ can stay for four weeks.

d) ☐ don't have to do sports.

5 Of the four people who wrote to the magazine, which one seems to be an addict?

Name: ____________________

6 One writer gives a reason why she/he isn't an addict. Who? What is the reason?

a) Name: ____________________

b) Reason: ____________________

7 Which writer probably improves his/her English with the internet? Explain your answer.

a) Name: ____________________

b) Because: ____________________

8 The text talks a lot about the problems of the internet, but it also mentions some positive things. List three.

____

____

2.2 Holiday activities

The six teenagers below live in Australia. They are looking for something to do during their holidays.

First read the statements about the people (0 – 5) and then read the adverts for some activities (A – G). Decide which activity would be best for each person. Write the correct letters in the grid below. There are more activities than people.

0	1	2	3	4	5
C					

0 Jack

"I'm crazy about sport. I play rugby and cricket, but I like water sports best of all. This year I'd like to do something different – perhaps even a little dangerous!"

1 Emily

"I live in Sydney, Australia's largest city. In my holidays, I like to get away from city life. I love animals and I enjoy being outdoors. I don't mind working in my holidays. It keeps me fit!"

2 Ryan

"I don't like spending much time with other people. I'm not one for group activities. I'd like to see more of my country, but I don't have a lot of money."

3 Olivia

"I'm not a sporty or musical person. But I'm quite artistic and creative. Last year I took a cookery course, but it wasn't a great success. I'd like to try something new this year."

4 Cooper

"I've always been fascinated by people and their cultures. I think it's important to meet and understand people with different lives or different origins. I'm also very interested in the history of Australia."

5 Chloe

"I have such a busy life, so on holiday I just want to relax and spend a couple of weeks on a sunny beach, perhaps take a boat trip, and have a nice meal in the evenings."

ACTIVITIES

A

Painting and photography

Australia has some of the most beautiful countryside and coastline you could ever hope to see. We can help you to show this in your own pictures. Learn with experts to paint and/or photograph. Weekend and summer courses. Lots of fun guaranteed!

Contact:
The Picture School, tel. (02) 4982 8567

B

Australia Wildlife Park Volunteer

This wonderful experience will allow you to learn all about Australian wildlife. Not only will you help with the daily tasks of feeding animals, you will also be part of special projects to help the environment. You will live in huts in the sanctuary and spend your working day out of doors.

A great adventure! Phone us for more information:
01892 701881

C

Adventure Out Recreation Programs are for individuals, groups and the whole family.

Have fun, learn new skills and increase your self-confidence! You can choose between one-day rock climbing trips, where you can learn the basics. Other programs include white-water rafting and our wonderful weekenders in Margaret River, which include camping, climbing, caving and abseiling—all in the one trip!

We offer safe, high quality adventure experiences in an environmentally responsible way.
Tel (08) 9472 3919 or **Fax** (08) 9472 3904

D

Aussie Explorer Bus Passes give you a wide choice of cheap bus travel options and can be used on Greyhound Pioneer and McCafferty's services. Aussie Explorer Bus Passes are ideal for the independent traveller – they are very flexible and allow unlimited stops on one route, for example from Adelaide to Alice Springs, or Brisbane to Sydney. Comfortable buses with modern facilities. The cheap and flexible way to see Australia.
For more information go to
http://www.holidaysallover.com.au/welcome/

E

Aboriginal Cultural Tours *in South East Australia*

The Aboriginal culture is one of the oldest on earth. Spend a week discovering the traditions, skills and beliefs that have been passed down from generation to generation. Meet with the Ngarrindjeri people and share some of their ancient culture.

Phone **1300 78 75 79** for more details.

F

Jazz Workshop

Do you play an instrument and want meet other young musicians to make music together? Jazz Workshop is the only music school in Sydney that specializes in jazz. We are offering school holiday workshops from June to September for young musicians aged 14 – 18. Individual and group lessons.

Contact us by email: info@jazzworkshop.au

G

Ocean View, Jurien Bay

Relax, do nothing, enjoy the sea and the sand. Jurien Bay is 250 km north of Perth. It's wonderful place to spend a week or two in the sunshine – the beaches are long, isolated and sandy. Take a cruise boat and see dolphins and whales, and in the evening visit one of the excellent local restaurants.
Ocean View, 4 Canberra Place, Jurien Bay, Western Australia, 6516

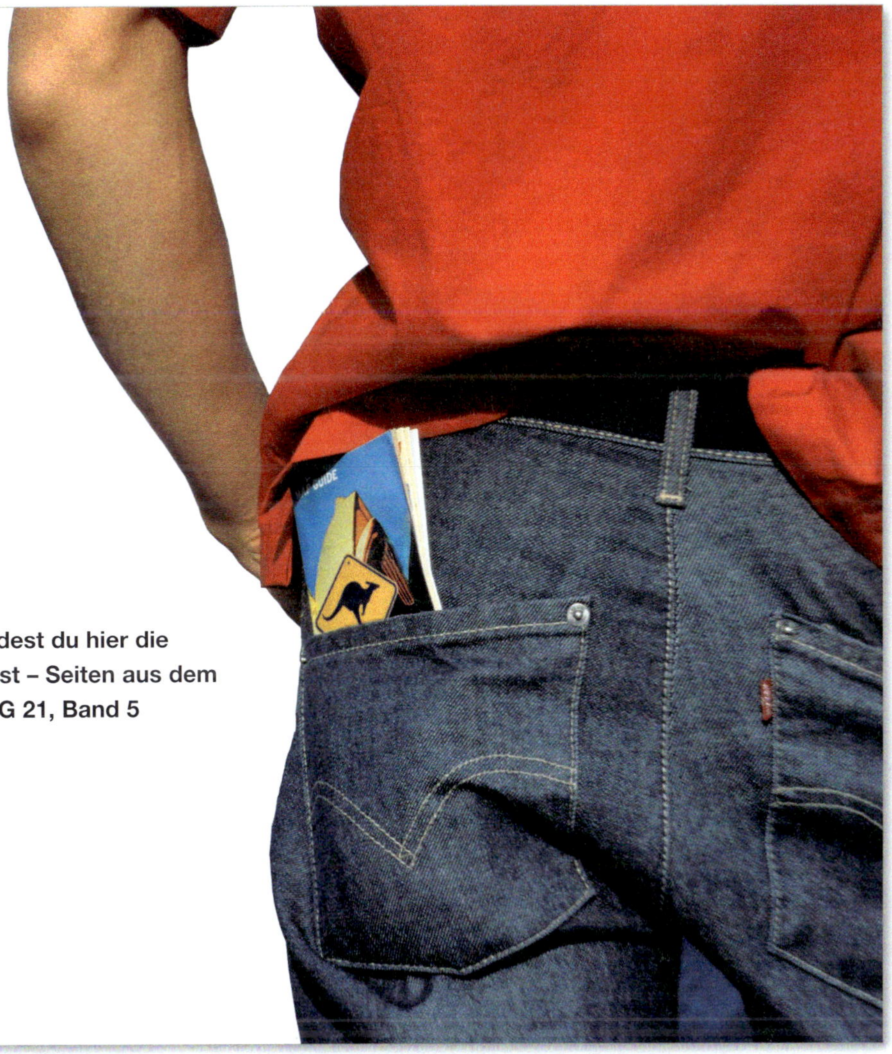

Zur Wiederholung findest du hier die Getting ready for a test – Seiten aus dem Schülerbuch English G 21, Band 5

1 WORDS Travelling on holiday

Fill in the right words to complete the sentences.

breakfast • (to) change planes • (to) check in • city centre • departure gate • key card • (to) land • meal • single ticket • suitcases • taxi • ticket machines

You're flying to Australia for a wonderful holiday! At the airport, you first (1) *check in*. Then you go to the (2) ... For your flight it's gate D21.

Now you're on the plane. The flight to Australia is very long and on the way you need to eat and drink. The flight attendant offers you a drink and a hot (3) ... There are lots of nice things on the menu today.

After you (4) ... at Singapore Airport, you finally (5) ... in Sydney. Of course, you hope that your (6) ... arrive too! If not, you'll have to go to the lost luggage office.

So how do you travel from the airport into the (7) ...? Well, the quickest and easiest way is to take a (8) ..., but it's also the most expensive one: it costs about 50 Australian dollars. So you decide to take a train instead. The (9) ... are easy to use and a (10) ... to the city is only 15 Australian dollars.

Now – tired but happy – you're at your hotel. The receptionist gives you the (11) ... to your room and tells you about the hotel – for example, the times when you can have (12) ... in the mornings.

2 Judy's job (Simple present and present progressive)

a) *Judy is the flight attendant who you can see in the photo above. Finish these sentences about her job. Use the* **simple present** *or the* **present progressive**.

1 Judy's job is exciting. She often ... (travel) to different countries.
2 Right now, she ... (fly) to Australia.
3 A typical day for Judy starts early. She usually ... (get up) at 5 o'clock. Then she ... (have) her breakfast and ... (drive) to the airport.
4 It is 10 o'clock now and Judy ... (work). She ... (bring) coffee and tea to the passengers on her plane.
5 Now it is 10 o'clock the next morning. Judy ... (just/arrive) at her hotel.
6 Judy always ... (stay) at a hotel when she is in another country. She ... (sleep) at the hotel – then the next day she ... (fly) home again.

b) *Write sentences about things that you often do and some things that you're doing right now.*
I often surf the internet. Right now, I'm chatting with my friends.

3 Australia's most dangerous animals (Simple past and past progressive)

Read the text about Australia's most dangerous animals on the right, then complete the two stories below. Use the simple past or past progressive of the verbs in brackets.

AUSTRALIA is home to some of the world's most dangerous animals. There are snakes, spiders and sometimes sharks. The most dangerous of all, however, are crocodiles. Two or three people die every year in crocodile attacks. Here are two stories about people who were attacked.

There's a crocodile in our tent!

In January 2005, two young Australians went camping near the Pentecost River in the north of Australia. At about 2 o'clock in the morning, they (1) *were sleeping* (sleep) when suddenly a crocodile (2) ... (come) into their tent. They (3) ... (run) to their car and (4) ... (climb) onto it. The next morning at 11 o'clock, they (5) ... (still/sit) on their car when some hunters (6) ... (arrive) and (7) ... (save) their lives.

Smile please!

In 2008, a tourist in Queensland was stupid – but lucky. He (8) ... (sit) in a boat on a river when a crocodile (9) ... (swim) towards the boat. The man's friend (10) ... (stand) on land. 'Put your hand in the water and play with the crocodile!' he (11) ... (shout). 'I'm going to take a photo.' Seconds later, the crocodile (12) ... (try) to bite the man's hand. 'It was a scary moment!', he (13) ... (say) afterwards.

4 WORDS It was scary! (Words that describe experiences)

a) *Look at the box with adjectives. Find five pairs of adjectives that mean (almost) the same: good – ...*

b) *Find at least eight pairs of adjectives that mean opposite things: amazing – bad; awesome – ...*

c) *Write about ten experiences. Use adjectives from the box:*

1) *Yesterday I played table tennis against my younger brother and lost 11–2. It was depressing!*
2) ...

amazing • awesome • awful • bad • boring • cool • crazy • dangerous • depressing • different • difficult • easy • excellent • exciting • fantastic • fine • funny • good • great • horrible • interesting • laughable • mad • nice • OK • sad • scary • silly • strange • surprising • terrible • unbelievable

5 WRITING One day last year ...

a) *Below is a very short story! Can you make it more interesting? Write the story again.*

Jake was riding his bike in the mountains. He fell off and broke his leg. He called for help with his mobile phone. Some people saved him. He went to hospital. He met Anne, a doctor. They fell in love. They got married.

When?	one day last year, last September, first, then, next, after that, finally, ...
Who?	the man/woman/people who ...
How?	quickly, slowly, suddenly, ... (really) amazing/awful; (feel) happy/sad, ...
Linking words	because, but, so (that), although, when, while, ...

b) *Compare your story with a partner's.*

1 LISTENING Travelling to Australia

oder Web-Code: EG21-B5-028

You are flying to Australia with your family. Listen to five announcements or short conversations that you hear on your journey.
- *Look at the questions below. You have 30 seconds.*
- *Listen and note down the right answer – A, B or C.*
- *You will hear all the recordings* ***once****.*

1 At Heathrow Airport in London you hear this announcement: 'Flight Q201 to Sydney is now boarding at ...'

A GATE 7 B GATE 17 C GATE 70

2 On the plane from London to Sydney, the flight attendant is offering you ...

A an omelette or pasta.

B chicken with a salad or pork chops.

C chicken with a salad or pasta.

3 At Sydney Airport one of your suitcases is missing! The lost luggage office is ...

A just over there. B on the first floor. C next to the passport office.

4 A taxi from the airport into the city costs ...

A AU$ 50 B AU$ 52.50 C AU$ 55.20

5 Now you are at your hotel. Tomorrow breakfast is from ...

A 06:00–10:00 B 06:30–9:30 C 07:00–10:30

2 LISTENING Shark attack!

oder Web-Code: EG21-B5-029

You are going to hear a radio news programme about how Jon Kerry, a young Australian, was attacked by a great white shark.

– *Look at the questions below for 30 seconds.*
– *Now listen and do the tasks. You will hear the news programme* **twice**.

a) *Which is right? Note down* A, B, C *or* D.

1 Jon was attacked near a beach in ...
A Queensland.
B South Australia.
C New South Wales.
D Western Australia.

2 When he was attacked, Jon was ...
A surfing.
B swimming.
C sunbathing.
D windsurfing.

3 The shark bit into Jon's ...
A arm.
B foot.
C shoulder.
D leg.

4 It held him for around ...
A 3.5 seconds.
B 5 seconds.
C 40 seconds.
D 5 minutes.

5 After the attack ...
A a boat saved Jon in the water.
B the shark pulled Jon to the beach.
C Jon swam back to the beach.
D a big wave carried Jon to the beach.

6 Jon thought this was the ... part.
A most exciting
B easiest
C scariest
D most painful

b) *Finish the sentences.*

1 Jon's friends probably saved his life when they ... a rope[1] round his ... and stopped the bleeding.
2 Jon is lucky. He will always have a big scar[2] but he ...
3 Experts say that sharks don't normally ...
4 The experts also say that more people die in accidents on the road in Australia ... than from shark attacks ...
5 You should always swim ... so your friends can help you. And never swim ... or ... because that's when sharks usually feed.

[1] rope [rəʊp] *Seil* [2] scar [skɑː] *Narbe*

3 LISTENING Young Australians and the internet

oder Web-Code: EG21-B5-030

Young Australians are among the world's biggest users of the internet. Six Australian students are discussing what they do online.

- *Look very carefully at the statements below for 30 seconds.*
- *Now listen and do the task.*
- *You will hear the recordings only **once**.*

Right or wrong? True or false? Note down 'T' or 'F'.

1 This student thinks that she spends too much time online.
2 This student never does just one thing at a time when he uses a computer.
3 This student thinks her parents don't care about what she does online.
4 This student thinks that young people know how to be safe online.
5 This student tells a story about something that happened to him.
6 This student thinks the internet is good for teenagers.

4 WRITING An online magazine for young Europeans

You often read an online magazine for young Europeans. This week, the magazine wants readers' ideas about the internet and it has a story competition.
Write about one of the two topics below. Write a text of about 150 words.

Topic 1: The internet and me
When and where do you usually use the internet? What do you do online? What things do you do most often online? Can the internet be bad for you?

Topic 2: A scary moment!
Finish this story in your own words.

It was a Saturday afternoon in September. I was bored, so I decided to go for a bike ride. After about an hour, I was on a small road in the country ...

How am I doing?

Check your answers to tasks 1–3 in the Answer key.

About the test

This test gave you the chance to try some of the kinds of tasks that you will do one day in your exam (*Abschlussprüfung*). If you found some tasks difficult, don't worry. You've got lots of time to practise. Remember: 'Practice makes perfect!'

Listening

The first three tasks in the test were listening tasks. The following questions will help you to think about how you did. Read the questions and tick the boxes that are right for you.

1 **How hard or easy was each task?**

	easy	OK	quite hard	very hard
Task 1	❑	❑	❑	❑
Task 2	❑	❑	❑	❑
Task 3	❑	❑	❑	❑

2 **What was difficult in the tasks?**

People spoke quickly. ❑
I found the accents difficult. ❑
There was a lot of information.
I couldn't find the exact answers. ❑
I didn't have time to write the answers to the questions. ❑
There were words and phrases that I just couldn't understand. ❑

3 **How did you do the tasks?**

I read the questions carefully first so I knew exactly what I had to listen for. ❑
I looked quickly at the questions first but only read them carefully while I was listening. ❑
I wrote as many answers as I could the first time I heard the text and checked them (or filled in gaps) the second time. ❑
There were lots of things I couldn't understand and I panicked. ❑

Writing

The fourth task in your test was a writing task. Work with a partner. Exchange the texts you've written and read your partner's text. Copy and fill in the assessment sheet[1] below. Remember: the idea is to help your partner with your feedback!

Assessment sheet				
Name of partner ...	☺	😐	☹	Comments
Did your partner ... *1* ... make grammar mistakes (with a tense, a plural form, etc.)?				
2 ... use interesting vocabulary or just easy words and phrases?				
3 ... write longer sentences with linking words or just short sentences?				
4 ... write a text that is clear and easy to understand?				

[1] assessment sheet *Beurteilungsbogen*

1 WORDS Free-time activities

What do you do in your free time? Are you sporty? Is running your hobby? Or do you like reading a good book?

a) *Work with a partner. How many free-time activities can you add to the list below?*

horse riding • drawing and painting • listening to music • playing a musical instrument • watching TV or DVDs • playing basketball • playing football • cycling • using a computer • reading books or magazines • relaxing • meeting friends • ...

b) *Look at your list and put the activities into groups.*

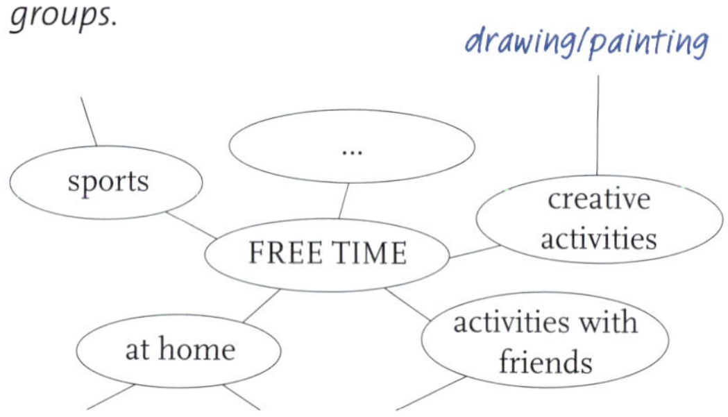

c) *Talk about all your free-time activities. Tell each other why you like/don't like doing them.*

A: I often go horse riding. I love horses and I think it's great to be with them every day.

B: Well, I don't agree. I think it's too much work. But I enjoy listening to music ...

2 WORDS Talking about films

You see this film review on an internet movie website. Find the missing words and phrases to complete the text.

(to) act • actor • drama • famous • main character • star • (to) take part in • talent • (to) tell the story • true events

Take the Lead *****

'Ballroom dancing meets New York's gangs'

The (1) *drama* *Take the Lead* (2) ... of Pierre Dulaine, a ballroom dance teacher, who goes to work in one of New York's most difficult inner city schools full of problem kids. *Take the Lead* is actually based on (3) ..., and Pierre Dulaine is, in fact, a real person. He still works with American teenagers around the USA and has become quite (4) ... after the film came out.

The (5) ... of the film is the Spanish American (6) ... Antonio Banderas. He plays the (7) ... Pierre Dulaine. When Dulaine first arrives in the school, the kids all think he is crazy. They are into hip hop, not classical dance. However, after Dulaine shows them a tango with another professional dancer, the kids start to get interested. The film ends when they all (8) ... a national ballroom competition.

The kids are all 'normal' American teenagers and had never (9)... before. But they are all great natural acting (10) ... and some of them are amazing hip hop dancers.

In 2006, *Take the Lead* won an award for 'Best Teen Movie.'

3 I'd love to be a movie star (Conditional sentences type 2)

Finish these sentences about being a famous movie star. All the sentences are conditional sentences type 2.

1 If a famous director *chose* (choose) me for one of his films, I*'d / would be* (be) famous too.
2 I ... (go) to Hollywood if I ... (become) a famous actor.
3 I ... (not live) here if I ... (be) rich.
4 If I ... (act) in a movie, all my friends ... (come) to see me.
5 If I ... (have) lots of money, I ... (buy) a yacht.
6 If I ... (play) a part in a movie, I ... (meet) famous actors every day on the film set.
7 But the problem is, if I ... (be) a movie star, I ... (not see) my family very often.
8 Perhaps I ... (not be) so happy if I ... (be) a film star!

4 SPEAKING Having a conversation

Talk to your partner for about two minutes about anything – films, magazines, music, what you did last weekend, the town where you live, ... The phrases below will help you.

starting a conversation	Hello. / Hi. / My name's ... / What's your name? / ...
likes and dislikes	I like / don't like ... / What about you? / And you? / ...
showing interest	Really? / Oh, that's interesting! / Sounds great! / Wow! / ...
agreeing	Yes, me too. / That's right! / Oh, I don't. / Sorry, I don't agree. / ...
asking questions	So when did you ...? / Why ...? / How long ...? / Where ...? / Sorry, can you say that again please? / ...
ending the conversation	See you again. / Bye!

5 WORDS Jim and Kate (Words that describe feelings)

***a)** Complete these sentences with words or phrases from the box on the right.*

angry • be afraid • be mad about sb./sth. • bored • confused • cool • different • excited • great • happy • independent • jealous • lonely • (to) look forward to sth. • nervous • proud • relaxed • responsible (for) • sad • safe • scared • shy • silly • strange • surprised • terrible • tired

1 Jim and Kate have been together for a month now and they ... still ... each other.
2 Kate was ... when Jim asked her if she'd like to date him. She thought he liked Laura.
3 Jim is usually very ..., so he wasn't even nervous on their first date.
4 But when Kate forgot his MP3 player on the bus last week, he was very ... with her.
5 Sometimes Kate is ... when Jim tries to be funny – his jokes are very strange!
6 At first she didn't want to meet Jim's parents as she always feels a bit ... with new people.
7 When Kate met her old boyfriend Pete at a party, Jim was a bit ... at first – until he saw that she wasn't interested in Pete any more.
8 They're ... the summer holidays this year: they're going to Canada for three weeks!

***b)** Write six sentences like these with words you haven't used in a).*

1 READING Choosing a book

These American high school students are in their English literature class. They have to choose a book to read. To help them, their English teacher has written short summaries of some books.

Look at the profiles of the five students and the seven book summaries below. Choose the best book for each student.

Answer: Student A – Book ...

Student A : Conrad

Conrad doesn't really enjoy reading short stories or novels, but he reads magazines. He loves sport and is also interested in music and skateboarding.

Student B : Brittany

Brittany has her own blog where she writes her thoughts. She is fascinated by young people, their loves and fears, their relationships, and their problems.

Student C : Jeanette

Jeanette loves reading stories. For her, a 'good book' is one where the characters have lots of real life adventures. She doesn't like fantasy or horror stories.

Student D : John Paul

John Paul is interested in football but the thing he likes best is computer games. He particularly loves fantasy games where 'anything is possible'.

Student E : Rikki

Rikki's family came to the U.S. from Puerto Rico. Now, as a teenager, he is interested in politics and wants to help people from ethnic minorities.

BOOK SUMMARIES

Fiction

1 **Dark Universe** Three teenage friends fall through a 'time hole' and find themselves in a parallel world where amazing and fantastic things happen. Can they survive – and will they ever return to their old lives?

2 **Something** Something is 'out there'. Waiting. Watching. Looking for you! VERY scary!

3 **Lola and the Detective Agency** When Lola and her friends discover a crime, nobody believes them. They have to set up their own detective agency to catch the criminals. Lots of action right up to the last page!

Non-fiction

4 **Voices from the fields** Fascinating interviews with migrant workers from Mexico who talk about their lives in the fields of California where they pick fruit.

5 **Strategies for teens** Being a teenager is not always easy but this book is full of great advice about families, boy/girlfriends and many other aspects of teen life.

6 **The Journey West** The book uses diaries, letters and old photos to tell the fascinating story of the long journeys to the West in America's history.

7 **Babe** Babe Ruth was probably the greatest baseball player who has ever lived. This biography tells the true story of his life. Wonderful descriptions of exciting games!

2 MEDIATION A note to your friend

Your American friend is staying with you in Germany at the moment. Your friend would like to know about some interesting things to do.

Read the brochure below and write a short note in English to your friend. Give the main points about the tours. Use the example on the right to help you.

Hi!
Hope you slept well. You wanted to know about some interesting things to do while I'm at school. I found out about some guided cycle tours that sound great. Here are the main points:

–

–

Erleben Sie die Stadt per Rad

Fahrrad-Stadtrundfahrten

Fahrrad-Rundfahrten durch die Stadt – für Gruppen von 10–15 Personen – begleitet von erfahrenen Stadtführern.

Sehen Sie unsere Stadt und ihre Attraktionen vom Fahrrad aus. Wir machen Halt an interessanten Punkten. Dort werden Sie Informationen über die Geschichte der Stadt und touristische Highlights erhalten.

Dauer
Unsere abwechslungsreiche Tour führt durchs Stadtzentrum und verschiedene Stadtteile und dauert ca. 120 Minuten, in denen wir etwa 12 km zurücklegen.

Abfahrt
März – September
täglich 10:00 und 14:00 Uhr.

Treffpunkt ist vor dem Informationszentrum neben der Liebfrauenkirche im Stadtzentrum (bei schlechtem Wetter im Informationszentrum).

Preise
€ 29,– pro Person inkl. Fahrradmiete
(Bei angemeldeten Gruppen mit mehr als 25 Teilnehmern € 22,50 pro Person.)

3 READING Dev Patel

This text is from an online British movie magazine. Read the whole article through first, then do the two tasks on the next page.

Meet Dev Patel, teenage movie star

The hit movie *Slumdog Millionaire* tells the story of 17-year-old Jamal, one of the millions of extremely poor people (the 'slumdogs') who live in the slums[1] of India's largest city, Mumbai. Jamal goes on the Indian TV gameshow *Who Wants to Be a Millionaire?*, answers all the questions correctly, wins the top prize – and finds the girl he loves. In 2009, the movie won eight Oscars. Its star was the young English actor Dev Patel …

WHEN Dev Patel arrived in Mumbai to film *Slumdog Millionaire*, it was only his second visit to India. In fact, learning the Mumbai accent was, he says, one of the hardest things he had to do. He wasn't a famous actor, either. He had liked drama very much at school in England, and he had played a small part in a British TV series, but that was all. So how did he become Jamal and what was it like when he was suddenly an international movie star?

Dev was born near London in 1993. His parents are Indians who had moved to England when they were young. His dad is a computer technician, his mum a carer[2].

Dev went to a 'typical' English secondary school. His first hobby was martial arts – karate then tae kwon do. He was excellent at both and even took part in the Youth Olympics. But after a role in a school play, Dev found that what he really loved was acting.

His mum wanted to encourage him, and when Dev was 14, she showed him a small advertisement in a newspaper. A TV company wanted people for a series called Skins, about a group of teenage friends. Dev wrote a reply – and got a part.

Three years later – Dev was 17 – the successful British film director Danny Boyle was looking for someone to play Jamal in *Slumdog Millionaire*. Mumbai is the home of the huge Indian movie industry. People sometimes call it Bollywood: Bombay (the old name for Mumbai) plus Hollywood. The problem was that young, male Bollywood actors are all very strong and handsome. Boyle wanted a young man who looked more like a 'slumdog'. It was Boyle's daughter who told her dad about Dev – she often watched Skins. Dev had five auditions[3] ('I was crying at the end because I didn't think I'd get the part', he says) but then he was Jamal.

For Dev, the next five months were like a dream. He was in Mumbai and on a movie set. With him were a world-famous director, some of the best known older Bollywood stars, real kids from the slums of Mumbai, and the beautiful young actress who is his girlfriend in the movie. 'I grew up five years in those five months,' Dev says.

What did the real people from Mumbai's slums think? Dev was amazed by them. They were so proud that they were in the movie. 'Don't tell people we're poor,' they said to Dev and Boyle. 'Tell them we're happy. We aren't poor because we're happy.'

[1] slum [slʌm] *Armenviertel* [2] carer ['keərər] *(Alten-)Pflleger/in* [3] audition [ɔː'dɪʃn] *Sprechprobe*

Questions on the text

a) *Choose the correct answer –* **A, B, C** *or* **D.**

1 What do you learn most about in this article?
- A the Indian movie industry.
- B the film *Slumdog Millionaire*.
- C the young English actor Dev Patel.
- D the life of the poor people in the slums of Mumbai.

2 The article says it was ... Dev Patel got the lead role in *Slumdog Millionaire*.
- A just a matter of time before
- B because of his good looks that
- C quite surprising that
- D decided very quickly that

3 In the movie, Dev plays the role of a young Indian man who ...
- A wins an Oscar.
- B becomes a millionaire.
- C moves to Mumbai.
- D tells a story.

4 Before he acted in the film *Slumdog Millionaire*, Dev ...
- A was already a famous actor.
- B had lived for a long time in Mumbai.
- C had only played a small role in a TV series.
- D could speak with a Mumbai accent.

5 Dev ...
- A has Indian parents but grew up in England.
- B has English parents and grew up in England.
- C has Indian parents and moved to England when he was small.
- D has English parents but grew up in India.

6 Which activity interested Dev most when he was at school?
- A tae kwon do
- B acting
- C the Youth Olympics
- D karate

7 How did Dev get the part in Skins?
- A His dad helped him.
- B A TV company wrote to him.
- C He often watched it on TV.
- D He replied to a newspaper advertisement.

b) *Finish the sentences with information from the text.*

8 Danny Boyle, the director of *Slumdog Millionaire*, chose Dev for the part of Jamal and not a young, male Bollywood actor because Dev ...

9 Mr Boyle found out about Dev from ...

10 At the end of his auditions, Dev was crying because ...

11 Filming *Slumdog Millionaire* in Mumbai changed Dev a lot. He describes this change when he tells us that ...

12 Dev expected the people who lived in the slums of Mumbai to be really sad. In fact, he found that although they are poor, ...

4 SPEAKING Talking about a picture

Partner A

Describe to your partner what you can see in this photo.
(Partner B: just listen).
Speak for around one minute.
- *Who are the people in the photo? Where are they? What are they doing?*
- *Describe their feelings.*
- *Would you like to be one of the people in the photo? Why (not)?*

Partner B

Now it's your turn. Describe to your partner what you can see in this photo.
(Partner A: just listen).
Speak for around one minute.
- *Who are the people in the photo? Where are they? What are they doing?*
- *Describe their feelings.*
- *Would you like to be one of the people in the photo? Why (not)?*

5 SPEAKING Hobbies and interests

Now talk to your partner. Tell each other about your hobbies and interests. Talk together for about three minutes. Here are some ideas:

- What do you like doing in your free time? Why?
- Where, when and how often do you do those things?
- Do you do them alone, with your family or with friends?
- Describe the last time you did one of the activities.
- Is there one thing that you hate doing?

How am I doing?

Check your answers to tasks 1 and 3 in the Answer key.

About the test

This second test gave you the chance again to try some of the kinds of tasks that you will do one day in your exam (*Abschlussprüfung*). This time, the tasks tested your reading, mediation and speaking skills. If you found some tasks difficult, don't worry. You've got lots of time to practise. Remember: 'Practice makes perfect!'

Reading

Task 1 and task 3 in the test were reading tasks. The following three questions will help you to think about how you did. Read the questions and tick the boxes that are right for you.

1 **How hard or easy was each task?**

	easy	OK	quite hard	very hard
Task 1	❑	❑	❑	❑
Task 2	❑	❑	❑	❑
Task 3	❑	❑	❑	❑

2 **What was difficult in the tasks?**

- The texts were quite long and complicated. ❑
- There were words and phrases that I just couldn't understand. ❑
- There was a lot of information. I couldn't find the exact answers. ❑
- The tasks weren't like the tasks that we do in class. ❑

3 **How did you do the tasks?**

- I always read the questions carefully so that I knew what to look for in the texts. ❑
- I tried to understand the main ideas of the text first. That helped me to guess words that I wasn't sure about. ❑
- If there was a question that I wasn't sure about, I left it out and came back to it later. ❑
- I scanned the text when I looked for a special piece of information. ❑
- I checked my answers at the end to make sure I hadn't made a 'silly' mistake. ❑

Speaking

1 Copy and fill in the assessment sheet below about your partner's presentation in the fourth task (Talking about a picture).

Assessment sheet				
Name of partner ...	☺	😐	☹	Comments
Did your partner ...				
1 ... speak clearly and loudly enough?				
2 ... find enough to say?				
3 ... answer all the questions?				
4 ... have problems finding the right words?				
5 ... make grammar or vocabulary mistakes?				

2 Now look at the checklist on the right and talk about how well you did in the fifth task, the dialogue about your hobbies and interests.

- We listened to each other. ❑
- We only gave short answers. ❑
- We showed interest in each other. ❑
- There was a good flow in our dialogue.[1] ❑

[1] There was a good flow in our dialogue. *Unser Gespräch verlief flüssig.*

Getting ready for a test 1

1 LISTENING Travelling to Australia

1 A Gate 17
2 C chicken with salad or pasta
3 A just over there
4 B $ 52.50
5 C 07:00–10:30

2 LISTENING Shark attack

a)
1 C New South Wales
2 A surfing
3 D leg
4 B 5 seconds
5 C Jon swam back to the beach
6 C scariest

b)
1 ... they **tied** a rope round his **leg** ...
2 ... but he **didn't lose his leg** / **survived** / **is alive**.
3 ... **attack** / **kill** people.
4 ... in Australia every **day** than from shark attacks **in ten years**.
5 ... always swim **in groups**, so your friends can help you. And never swim **in the early morning or in the evening** ...

3 LISTENING Young Australians and the internet

1 False
2 True
3 False
4 True
5 True
6 True

4 WRITING An online magazine for young Europeans

(individuelle Lösungen)

Getting ready for a test 2

1 READING Choosing a book

1 Student A – Book 7
2 Student B – Book 5
3 Student C – Book 3
4 Student D – Book 1
5 Student E – Book 4

2 MEDIATION A note to your friend

(individuelle Lösungen)

3 READING Dev Patel

a)
1 C the young English actor Dev Patel
2 C quite surprising that
3 B becomes a millionaire.
4 C had only played a small role in a TV series.
5 A has Indian parents but grew up in England.
6 B acting
7 D He replied to a newspaper advertisement.

b)
8 ... looked more like a 'slumdog'
9 ... his daughter.
10 ... he didn't think he'd get the part.
11 ... he grew up five years in five months.
12 ... they are happy.

4 SPEAKING Talking about a picture

(individuelle Lösungen)

5 SPEAKING Hobbies and interests

(individuelle Lösungen)

Test three

3.1 Buy Nothing Day

The text below is a brochure.

First read the whole text. Then read the tasks.
Read the text again and do the tasks. Tick the correct box or write down the correct answer.

BUY NOTHING DAY

YOUR CHANCE TO STOP SHOPPING

What is Buy Nothing Day?

BND is a day when people can show what they think about our modern consumer society by buying nothing for 24 hours.

Why Buy Nothing Day?

FACT: Twenty per cent of the world's population consumes 86 per cent of the world's natural resources[1]. That leaves just 14 per cent for the four or five billion people in the world's poorer countries. Here in the richer countries, we have to ask ourselves: Do we need all the stuff we buy? When is "enough enough"?

When is it?

In Canada and the USA, BND takes place every year the day after the American holiday called 'Thanksgiving', near the end of November. It is the biggest shopping day of the year in the USA. In Europe and some other countries, BND comes on the last weekend in November, the time when lots of people are thinking about their Christmas shopping.

Where does it happen?

Buy Nothing Day now takes place in around 65 countries all over the world. Last year, over 1 million people took part. One of the places where BND is most popular is Europe.

What can I do?

There is no one central organisation for Buy Nothing Day. It is organised in different countries by different people – consumer groups[2], environmentalists and others. To take part, find out about what happens in your country – you will find details on the Internet. There will be lots of different activities on the day, so you should find something for you! Or just stay at home and don't shop!

How it all began

Buy Nothing Day was first started by a Canadian, Ted Dave. That was back in 1992. He worked in advertising, and it was his idea to protest against the message that the advertising industry always gives us: Buy more! In 1995, another organisation took up Dave's ideas. They're called 'Adbusters' and you can find out more about them on the Internet too.

Did you know ...?

What we spend every year

- In Europe: $11 billion on ice cream
- In Europe and the USA: $17 billion on pet food
- Worldwide: $33 billion on make-up and perfume

What money would buy in poorer countries

- $10 billion: clean drinking water for everyone in the world
- $1.3 billion: immunising[3] all children in the Third World
- $5 billion: universal literacy[4]

1 ***natural resources*** *Rohstoffquellen*
2 ***consumer group*** *Verbrauchergruppe*
3 ***to immunise*** *impfen*
4 ***literacy*** *Lese- und Schreibfähigkeit*

1 The main aim of Buy Nothing Day is to

a) ☐ ask people for money.
b) ☐ stop people buying products from poorer countries.
c) ☐ protest against the consumer society.
d) ☐ celebrate Thanksgiving.

2 Buy Nothing Day takes place on the same day

a) ☐ everywhere.
b) ☐ in Canada and the US.
c) ☐ in Europe and Canada.
d) ☐ in Europe and the US.

3 Over one million Europeans took part last year in BND.

This statement is **true** ☐ **false** ☐

The text says ______________________________

4 Buy Nothing Day was started in 1992.

This statement is **true** ☐ **false** ☐

The text says ______________________________

5 Buy Nothing Day is organized worldwide by

a) ☐ different people.
b) ☐ Ted Dave.
c) ☐ Adbusters.
d) ☐ consumers.

6 With $5 billion, poorer countries could

a) ☐ buy enough ice-cream for everyone.
b) ☐ feed their pets.
c) ☐ immunise all children.
d) ☐ teach everyone to read and write.

7 What do the following numbers refer to in the text?

20 ______________________________

____

65 ______________________________

____

1995 ______________________________

33 ______________________________

1.3 ______________________________

3.2 Magazines

The six teenagers below have different interests and hobbies. They are looking for interesting magazines.

First read the statements about the teenagers (0 – 5) and then read the descriptions of the magazines (A – G). Decide which magazine would be best for each person. Write the correct letters in the grid below. There are more magazines than people.

0	1	2	3	4	5
B					

0 Jessica

"I do a lot of sports in my free time, but best of all I like going to the cinema, or watching DVDs at home. I'm crazy about films and the world of films."

1 Ethan

"I love travelling, and if I can't travel myself, I enjoy reading about faraway places and other people's holidays."

2 Aaron

"I like playing computer games, but my main interest is football. I'm crazy about it. I play on my school team, and I go to watch my favourite team play whenever I can. But I'm not really interested in any other sports."

3 Caitlin

"I play the electric guitar in a rock band, and I'd like to play professionally one day. I listen to music every day, and go to concerts whenever I can."

4 Megan

"I'm not interested in sport or fashion. I'm interested in nature, animals, birds and faraway places."

5 Daniel

"I spend a lot of my free time on the computer. I got an X-Box for Christmas and since then my favourite activity is playing computer games. I'm always looking for something new."

MAGAZINES

A

SPORTS REPORT

The best weekly magazine for all your sports news. Whatever your interests – soccer, tennis, squash, cricket, canoeing – we keep you up-to-date. News of all the latest developments in the world of sport, and interviews with the people that matter. This is the magazine for all sports fans.

B

Hi!

Want to know the latest about your favourite movie, TV and music stars? Who's dating, married, divorced? Who wore what at the Academy Awards? Lots of news and photos. The latest fashion and beauty tips from Hollywood. *Hi!* has it all. Plus cooking, travel and the best horoscopes anywhere.

C

GAMES WORLD

Games World is the most popular magazine for gamers everywhere. With reviews of new computer games, articles about the world of computer gaming, and information about the latest hardware and software, this is the magazine you need to keep up-to-date.

D

KICK

Your monthly football magazine. Photos, interviews and analysis of all the latest matches. Training and diet tips for players. Player and team profiles, scores, league tables and more. Covers all professional UK teams plus worldwide football news. The ultimate magazine for football players and fans.

E

SPINNERS

Get the dates of all the concerts, festivals and gigs around the country.
Read interviews with your favourite singers and musicians – this month features Patty Smith. Read our reviews of the latest CDs and DVDs from the world of rock.

F

THE TRAVEL MAG

From weekend shopping holidays in New York City to beach holidays in the Caribbean, *The Travel Mag* brings you all the latest news and helps you to find your perfect holiday at the best price. Plus features about countries and cities around the world, and readers' holiday stories.

G

OUR WORLD

The magazine for nature lovers. Photos, maps, news stories, reports about the world we live in. Articles in this month's magazine include: 50 Ways to See Alaska, Killer Whales, The Power of the Wind – and many more.

TEST FOUR

4.1 Barack Obama

The text below is from an American magazine.

First read the whole text. Then read the tasks.
Read the text again and do the tasks. Tick the correct box or write down the correct answer.

1 ______________________________

Barack Obama made history on November 4th, 2008 when he won the presidential election in the USA. He is the first African-American to win the race for the White House. Obama's charisma, intelligence, and powerful speeches have made him extremely popular, not only with many Americans, but also with people from many other countries. He has been very successful with his message for change and his positive slogan: „Yes, we can."

2 ______________________________

Barack Obama was born in Hawaii in 1961 to a black Kenyan father and white American mother. In 1963 his parents divorced, and his mother married an Indonesian man. Barack's family moved to Indonesia in 1967. He attended schools in Jakarta until he was ten years old, when he returned to Hawaii to live with his grandparents. He saw his biological father only once after his parents divorced. His father died in a car accident in 1982; his mother died in 1995.

3 ______________________________

Barack studied political science and international relations at Columbia University in New York. After four years in New York, he moved to Chicago. There, from 1985 to 1988, he worked as director of a community project to set up job training and education programmes for poor people. He entered Harvard Law School in 1988 and graduated in 1991. Barack taught law at the University of Chicago Law School for twelve years.

4 ______________________________

In 1988 Barack met his wife, Michelle, an African-American lawyer from Chicago, while they were both working for a law firm there. Michelle's great-great-grandfather[2] was a slave in South Carolina. Barack and Michelle have two daughters, Malia and Sasha.

5 ______________________________

In 1996 Barack Obama became an Illinois senator and helped to make new laws for better health care and better education for the poor. In 2004 Obama was elected to the U.S. Senate – one of the very few African American Senators in U.S. history so far. In November 2008 he defeated John McCain to become America's 44th President after a very hard campaign battle.

1 ***low income*** *niedriges Einkommen*
2 ***great-great-grandfather*** *Ur-Urgroßvater*

1 Find the missing headlines for paragraphs 1–5. Write letters above each paragraph. There is one headline more than you need.

A	Political career	**D**	2008 presidential campaign
B	Barack's success	**E**	Early life
C	Education and career	**F**	Personal life and family

2 Which of the following statements about Barack Obama is not true.

a) ☐ He is the first African-American president of the USA.
b) ☐ He is popular at home and abroad.
c) ☐ His great-great grandfather was a slave.
d) ☐ Americans like his message for change.

3 Name four places where Barack Obama lived between 1961 and 1988.

______________________ ______________________

______________________ ______________________

4 Barack Obama saw his biological father only once

a) ☐ between 1961 and 1982.
b) ☐ until he was ten years old.
c) ☐ between 1963 and 1982.
d) ☐ after he married Michelle.

5 Where did Barack Obama study?

a) ☐ University of Chicago Law School
b) ☐ Columbia University
c) ☐ University of South Carolina
d) ☐ University of Illinois

6 The aim of the Chicago community project that Obama directed was

a) ☐ to make new laws for better health care.
b) ☐ to help poor people find homes.
c) ☐ to teach poor people law.
d) ☐ to help poor people get more education and better jobs.

7 Where did Barack Obama meet his wife Michelle?

a) ☐ In Chicago.
b) ☐ In South Carolina.
c) ☐ In New York.
d) ☐ Not in the text.

8 Name four jobs that Barack Obama has done in his life.

______________________ ______________________

______________________ ______________________

9 Fill in the gaps with the correct nationality.

Barack Obama's mother was ______________________, his father was

______________________, and his step-father was ______________________.

10 What do these numbers in the text refer to?

4 ______________________

10 ______________________

1982 ______________________

12 ______________________

44 ______________________

4.2 Books

The six teenagers below like reading different kinds of books.

First read the statements about the teenagers (0 – 5) and then read the book adverts (A – G). Decide which book would be best for each person. Write the correct letters in the grid below. There are more book adverts than people.

0	1	2	3	4	5
C					

0 Harry ...

never reads novels. He is only interested in science – especially in the environment.

1 Charlie ...

enjoys science-fiction. He likes to imagine what life could be like in the future or in a different world.

2 Sophie ...

loves reading and going to the cinema. She likes reading the book when she has seen the film. Her favourites are romantic novels.

3 Lucy ...

has always been interested in history and far-away places. She prefers stories about real people and their lives.

4 Will ...

likes fantasy and horror. He doesn't have time to read long books and prefers short stories.

5 Jessica ...

likes reading stories about people, their feelings and relationships. But she also enjoys a bit of adventure in her books.

BOOK ADVERTS

A

STAYING FAT FOR SARAH BYRNES *by Chris Crutcher*

Because of his great weight, Eric "Moby" Calhoune is a complete outsider at school. He forms a friendship with Sarah Byrnes, a burn victim. The friendship is tested by Sarah's inability to face the past and her relationship with her father – one of the most horrible characters in literature. Soon things get dangerous for both Moby and Sarah. Read the book and find out what happens.

B

Vampire Academy *by Richelle Mead*

Rose, half-human/half-vampire, and her best friend Lissa ran away from St. Vladimir's Academy, but now they have been caught and sent back. School means enemies, bullying and threats. How can Rose keep her friend safe? 332 pages of fantasy and horror. A dark novel by a talented young author – Mead's view of vampires is fresh and new.

C

Dr Art's Guide to Planet Earth

BY ART SUSSMAN

A book for people of all ages who are interested in the earth's life systems. Dr Sussmann makes it clear why we must learn to respect our planet, and stop treating it badly before it is too late.
Art's Guide is for "earthlings aged 12 to 120" – buy a copy for your kids, but don't forget to read it, too!

D

PRETTY MONSTERS *by Kelly Link*

This is Link's first book for young adults. In the first story, Miles wants to get back some poems that he buried[1] with his dead girlfriend, but he digs up the wrong body. The person comes back to life. And this is only one of nine stories that are funny and frightening, wonderful and macabre. Buy this book – buy two and give one to someone you really like.

1 **bury** *begraben*

E

The Giver *by Lois Lowry*

Jonas is born into a world where nobody is poor; where there is no crime or violence. All negative aspects of life have been eliminated. Everything is well organized and planned. At the age of twelve Jonas begins training for his future career, taught by the 'Giver'. Everyone seems to have forgotten what freedom and choice are all about. But the Giver has not forgotten. There is a price, but Jonas refuses to pay it ...

F

P.S. I love you

by Cecelia Ahern

Set in Ireland, Holly Kennedy is beautiful, smart and married to Gerry, the love of her life. When Gerry dies, she is lost. But before he died, Gerry wrote Holly 10 letters. The messages are Gerry's way of informing Holly that life goes on – and he will always be always by her side. A talented first novel, now a major movie starring Hilary Swank.

G

RED AZALEA *BY ANCHEE MIN*

An honest and frightening memoir of growing up in Communist China during 1960s and 1970s. Min describes her Shanghai childhood and later teen years on a work farm – years of backbreaking workdays and lonely nights. Min's autobiography is not just a growing-up story or a history lesson, it is a story of strength and courage.

Test five

5.1 The power of nature

First read the whole text. Then read the tasks.
Read the text again and do the tasks. Tick the correct box or write down the correct answer.

We all know about the power of earthquakes that make huge buildings fall, and the power of waterfalls such as Niagara Falls, where every minute enough water crashes down to fill 50 Olympic swimming pools. We know about hurricanes, forest fires, floods[1] and tidal waves like the tsunami. But Mother Nature still has some surprises for us. Here are some of them.

A

The fastest wind
In 1999 in Oklahoma City the fastest wind speed ever – 318 miles (511 kilometres) an hour – was recorded. Winds of 70 miles (112 kilometres) an hour can blow away cars and houses. At 318 miles an hour they can derail[2] trains and tear up trees and sidewalks.

B

The biggest hailstones[3]
A long time ago hundreds of people were killed at the same time in the Himalayas. For ten centuries the cause of their death remained a mystery. Scientists have now discovered that they were killed by hailstones the size of baseballs.

C

It's raining frogs
Small frogs rain down on a town in Serbia and people run for shelter. Strong winds and heavy rain can pick up small animals and carry them for hundreds of miles. When the rain stops, the animals fall to the ground. There are stories of "fish rain" in coastal towns or on islands – for example in the Honduras, where they celebrate the "Rain of Fish Festival". People pick up the fish, take them home, cook them and eat them.

D

The longest wave on earth
Twice a year, between the months of February and March, the Atlantic Ocean waters roll up the Amazon river in Brazil and create the longest wave on earth. The phenomenon is known as the Pororoca. The waves can be up to 12 feet (3.6 metres) and can last for over half an hour. A surfer's dream.

E

Black Sun
During spring in Denmark, about one hour before the sun goes down, millions of birds fill the sky. It happens when the birds are on their way back from the south, where they spend the winter, to the north, where they spend the warmer months. They spend the days looking for food, and in the evenings they gather in groups to sleep. In Denmark this phenomenon is called "Black Sun".

1 ***flood*** *Überschwemmung*
2 ***derail*** *entgleisen*
3 ***hailstone*** *Hagelkorn*

1 Three natural phenomena to do with water are mentioned in the first paragraph. What are they?

______________________ ______________________ ______________________

2 Winds of 112 kilometres an hour can

a) ☐ tear up sidewalks.

b) ☐ derail trains.

c) ☐ blow away cars.

d) ☐ tear up trees.

3 For how many years did the cause of death of the people in the Himalayas remain a mystery?

For ______________________ years.

4 Which of the following statements is true?

a) ☐ Sometimes frogs and fish fall out of the sky.

b) ☐ It is a mystery how it can rain frogs or fish.

c) ☐ "Fish rain" only happens in the Honduras.

d) ☐ "Frog rain" is impossible.

5 At the "Rain of Fish Festival" people cook and eat fish. Where does the fish come from?

____

6 Why is the Pororoca a "surfer's" dream"?

____

7 Which of the following statements is **not** true?

a) ☐ Millions of birds come to Denmark in the spring.

b) ☐ Million of birds leave Denmark in the winter.

c) ☐ The birds gather in groups to sleep.

d) ☐ The sun in Denmark turns black in the spring.

8 Five people are watching different TV programmes about the natural phenomena mentioned in the text. Which one of the phenomena are they talking about?

Jack: "That's amazing. There are millions of them. Look, the sky is turning black."

____

Jill: "Look, there are trees flying through the air. It's unbelievable!"

____

Oliver: "I wonder how they managed to solve the mystery."

____

Sandy: "Perhaps the Serbs have a celebration, too."

____

Jim: "I'll think I'll go there with my surfboard next March."

____

5.2 A place to live

The six people below are all looking for somewhere to live.

First read the statements about the people (0 – 5) and then read the adverts below (A – G).
Decide which place would be best for each person to live. Write the correct letters in the grid below.
There are more places than people.

0	1	2	3	4	5
D					

0 Ruby

"I love cities as there is so much to do. There's only me and my cat, so I don't need a big place, but I do need an extra room for guests. A balcony would be nice, too."

1 Oliver

"I love gardening – the bigger the garden, the better for me. And we have three kids and a dog, so we need lots of space. We have two cars, so it's no problem to live outside the city and drive in every day."

2 Tom

"I'm a student and I don't have much money. I always eat at the university, and in the evenings I'm usually out with my friends, so I only need a room where I can sleep and study."

3 Lily

"We live in the centre of town and it's our dream to have a nice little place in the country for the weekends – with a small garden and at least two bedrooms. Perhaps something old and romantic."

4 Daniel

"Now we have a second child, we are looking for a modern house with three bedrooms. We want to stay in town so that we're near schools and shops. I'd like a big kitchen as I love cooking."

5 Anne

"When I was a child, we lived near the sea. I've lived in the city for over 30 years because my job was here. Next year I'll stop working. Finally I can move back to the seaside – if I can find a flat suitable for a single woman."

PLACES TO LIVE

A

Life in the country:

house on the outskirts of Manchester. Large living room, hall and kitchen, four bedrooms, two bathrooms. Beautiful, large garden. Double garage.

For more information call: 0161 554367

B

Country cottage[1]*:*

30 miles from Oxford in beautiful countryside. Building from the 19th century. Living room with open fireplace, hall, kitchen, two bedrooms, one bathroom. Small rose garden. Interested?

Contact: King & Mills 01865 19763

1 *cottage* *kleines Landhaus*

C

Large house in the centre of Manchester:

Living room, hall, four bedrooms, large kitchen.
Built 1920.
City house.
No garden.

For more information contact: 0161 6277613

D

2-bedroom flat

in a quiet side-street in Central London. Small living room, bathroom, kitchen and balcony.
Five minutes on foot to cinemas, theatres and restaurants.
Ideal for a single person. Animals welcome.

Contact: 0845 249 7337

E

New!

15 new houses will be ready in May. Suitable for young families. Only ten minutes to the town centre. Each house has a large living room and kitchen, 2 – 4 bedrooms, a small garden and parking lot.

For more information call 0845 542 614135

F

Near Brighton

Flat for sale. One bedroom, small living room and kitchen, bathroom, balcony. Ideal for a single person. Only five minutes walk to the sea.

For more information contact Miles Property Agency, 01273 3497199

G

Low-priced single room

in the city centre. Ideal as study-bedroom.
No kitchen. Shared bathroom. Gas heating.
No animals allowed.

Call 0161 997762 after 6 p.m.

Teil II

Leseverstehen – Wortschatz – Schreiben

Test one

1.1 Leseverstehen: Tom's blog

Tom is one of many British teenagers who have an Internet blog (or weblog). In this post he is writing about a recent holiday in Canada and the USA.

Read the whole text and then the tasks. Read the text again and do the tasks.
In tasks 1–4 tick the correct answer. In tasks 5–8 decide if the statements are true, false or if there is no information in the text.

I've just come back from the coolest, the most brilliant, the most totally AMAZING holiday I've ever had! Ten days in Canada and the USA with Mum, Dad and my sister Louise. This was my first trip to North America – and I must go back! The thing you read all the time, but never actually believe until you're there, is that these countries are just SO BIG! You can't "see" them in a few days. Here are a few notes about the holiday. If you want to see some pictures as well, then go to my Gallery Page.

How's your geography? Yeah – mine too! So here's a map to help.

Thursday 25th August Arrived in Montreal, Canada, after nearly 12 hours on the plane. Slept! Felt a lot better the next morning and the hotel was really nice. Montreal is quite old and – very French! Yes, here we were in Canada and everyone was speaking French. Fortunately, they all speak English too.

Saturday 27th August We had hired a car for the ten days of our holiday, and on Saturday we drove south into the USA. I was really excited. We stopped Saturday night in a small town called Lincoln. Everyone was so friendly – some kids outside the hotel asked me if I wanted to play baseball. When I said I was from England, they were really interested! We talked for about half an hour.

Sunday 28th August On south to Boston. I'd learned so much about Boston in history lessons at school (the Tea Party, Independence and all that), I couldn't believe I was here now. You can still see all the famous old buildings, but they're next to skyscrapers. It looks funny.

Tuesday 30th August OK, Boston was interesting, but this was the part of the holiday I'd been really waiting for: New York! We arrived late afternoon and crossed the Brooklyn Bridge – the one you see in all the photos. And then there it was: skyscrapers, yellow taxis, people everywhere. The place is crazy. There just don't seem to be any rules! Then you start to "go with the flow" and it's fantastic. I could have stayed here until the end of the holiday, but ...

Thursday 1st September ... we drove north again. Spent the night in a horrible motel in a little place called Binghamton, then on Friday drove to Buffalo and spent the day visiting Niagara Falls. Yes, *the* Niagara Falls! I loved it, but there were loads of tourists.

Saturday 3rd September The holiday was almost over but there was time to see just one more place before flying home. Back in Canada, we stayed Saturday and Sunday in Toronto. It's really modern – and after the USA, it seemed clean and quiet. The most famous thing here is the CN Tower, the world's tallest building. Right at the top there's a glass floor! Scary but fun! On Sunday evening, we dropped off our hire car at Toronto airport and boarded our plane for London. Goodbye Canada and the States – until next time.

1 Which of the following statements is true?

a) ☐ Tom has been to Canada and the US before.

b) ☐ Tom has posted some pictures of his holiday on the internet.

c) ☐ Tom went to Canada and the US with some friends.

d) ☐ Tom didn't enjoy his holiday in Canada and the US.

2 Who does Tom write his blog for?

a) ☐ Himself – it's his diary.

b) ☐ His friends.

c) ☐ His family.

d) ☐ Anyone who wants to read it.

3 What surprised Tom a bit about Montreal?

a) ☐ Everyone spoke French.

b) ☐ Everyone spoke English.

c) ☐ It was quite old.

d) ☐ The hotel was really nice.

4 Which statement best describes Tom's impression of New York?

a) ☐ He was disappointed.

b) ☐ He thought it was a frightening place.

c) ☐ He was a bit shocked at first but then he loved it.

d) ☐ He was glad to leave the city behind.

	true	false	not given
5 Tom has a pen friend in Canada.	☐	☐	☐
6 The holiday lasted ten days.	☐	☐	☐
7 Tom knew nothing about Boston until he went there.	☐	☐	☐
8 Tom went on a guided tour in Toronto.	☐	☐	☐

1.2 Wortschatz: Tom's blog

After they returned from Canada and the USA, Tom's sister wrote about their holiday as part of a school project. These sentences are taken from her project.

Fill in suitable words, or tick the correct box.

Our holiday in Canada and the USA

1 My brother Tom and I both think that this holiday was the best one we have ... had.

a) ☐ always
b) ☐ sometimes
c) ☐ ever
d) ☐ already

2 It was absolutely ...

a) ☐ terrible.
b) ☐ marvellous.
c) ☐ boring.
d) ☐ excited.

3 We ... from London to Montreal.

a) ☐ flow
b) ☐ fly
c) ☐ flowed
d) ☐ flew

4 The ... took twelve hours.

a) ☐ trip
b) ☐ travel
c) ☐ fly
d) ☐ way

5 We ... Montreal Airport early in the morning.

a) ☐ arrived
b) ☐ arrived at
c) ☐ landed
d) ☐ came on

6 The first thing we did was to

________________ a car for the ten days of our holiday.

7 We ... in Montreal for two nights in a really nice hotel.

a) ☐ stood
b) ☐ lived
c) ☐ stayed
d) ☐ visited

8 Canada and the USA are much bigger

________________ I had imagined.

9 On the way south to Boston, we stopped at a small place called Lincoln. There, some

kids were having a ________________ of baseball.

10 They were really friendly, ... when they heard that we were from England.

a) ☐ usually
b) ☐ extra
c) ☐ finally
d) ☐ especially

11 After Boston we went to New York City and we saw the ... buildings I have ever seen.

a) ☐ tallest
b) ☐ most tall
c) ☐ glass
d) ☐ awesome

12 We visited Niagara Falls, but there were too

________________ tourists.

13 We ________________ our last day in Toronto.

14 On Saturday 3rd September we returned to

London ________________ plane.

1.3 Schreiben: Tom's blog

Read the tasks carefully. Write complete sentences. Make sure you write about all the aspects in each task.

1 Write a short summary of Tom's holiday in North America. Write about 80 words.
- Say what he did.
- Say what he liked and didn't like.
- Describe Tom's feelings about his holiday.

2 You have an email from a penfriend called Sue. Tell her about the best holiday you have had. Write at least 100 words.

Posteingang

Von: Sue Davidson

Betreff: Holidays

Dear ...,

Thanks for your last email. I'm glad you liked my holiday photos. I can only say again – the holiday was fantastic, the best I've ever had. What about you? What's the best holiday you've ever had?

Sorry, must go now. Homework to do ☹

Lots of love
Sue

An: s.davidson@hotmail.com

Betreff: Holidays

Hi Sue,

You asked me in your last email about the best holiday I've ever had.
Well, I think that was ...

3 Some people say that when you spend only a few days in a country as a tourist, you can't see the place or the people as they really are.
What is your opinion? Is it worth visiting other countries as a tourist?
Give some pros and cons of travel. Write at least 120 words.

Test two

2.1 Leseverstehen: Roses and Mobiles

This is a short story set in modern-day Australia.

Read the whole text and then the tasks. Read the text again and do the tasks.
In tasks 1–4 tick the correct answer. In tasks 5–8 decide if the statements are true, false or if there is no information in the text.

Roses and Mobiles

Valentine's Day, February 14th, is a special day for lovers everywhere ...

"G'day," said the girl in the flower shop. "How may I help you?" "Oh, er, hi", said Nick. "I'd like those roses, please." And added: "For my sweetheart." Nick looked at the girl. She had the most beautiful eyes he had ever seen. As she walked past him to get the flowers, he read her name on her name badge[1]. Toni, it said. Toni Goddard. "There you are," said the girl. "I hope your sweetheart likes them." She smiled a beautiful smile. Nick paid and left. The girl watched him. He was tall, good-looking, athletic ... "What a great guy," she thought. "It's a pity he already has a sweetheart. Oh well, that's the story of my life."

Outside the shop, Nick looked at his watch. Nine o'clock. Time for work.

At 4 o'clock, Toni closed the flower shop. Things had not been good between her and Martin for some time, but he had invited her to dinner in a nice restaurant this evening, and she needed to buy him a Valentine's Day present. She hurried to the big department store in Sydney's Harbour Street, and took the elevator to the fifth floor where the electronics department was.

"G'day," she said to the man behind the counter. "I'd like ..." The man turned round. It was the guy from this morning. "Hi," he said with a big smile. "How may I help you – it's Toni, isn't it? I'm Nick. Nick Bensley." "Oh, er, Nick, hi. I'd like a mobile phone, please" said Toni. And added: "For my fiancé[2]." The smile disappeared from Nick's face. So, she had a fiancé. "Well, we have lots of those," he said at last. "I'll take that one," said Toni quickly. "Can you get me on to a network straight away?" "No worries[3]," said Nick. "A couple of minutes and it'll be ready to use." He came back with the phone and gave it to Toni. "I hope your fiancé likes it," he said.

Later that evening, Toni and Martin were in the restaurant. "I'm so sorry," Martin was saying. "But you have to agree things haven't been too good between us for a long time now, Toni. I think we should break it off. It just isn't going to work."

It was then that the mobile phone in Toni's bag rang. She hadn't yet given it to Martin. She was surprised. Who knew the number? But she was even more surprised when she looked across the restaurant. There, at another table, was Nick. He was holding up a mobile phone. "Martin, I'm sorry but I have to take this call," said Toni. He nodded. Quickly, Toni went to the corner of the room and answered the phone. It was a text message. It read: "Dearest Toni. I've thought about U all day. Do U really love another? Say U don't! Please be mine. PS: My 'sweetheart' is my sister."

With shining eyes and trembling[4] hands, Toni typed these words and pressed SEND: "I'm yours!"

1 ***name badge*** *Namensschild*
2 ***fiancé*** *Verlobter*
3 ***no worries*** *(Australian English) kein Problem*
4 ***to tremble*** *zittern*

1 Which of the following statements is **not** true?

a) ☐ Nick bought some roses.

b) ☐ Toni was wearing a badge with her name on it.

c) ☐ Nick thought Toni had beautiful eyes.

d) ☐ Nick forgot to pay for the flowers.

2 Where did Nick and Toni meet for the second time?

a) ☐ In a department store.

b) ☐ In a restaurant.

c) ☐ In a mobile phone shop.

d) ☐ In the flower shop where Toni worked.

3 Who answered the mobile phone when it rang in the restaurant?

a) ☐ Martin

b) ☐ Toni

c) ☐ Nick

d) ☐ Nick's sister

4 Who had Nick bought the roses for?

a) ☐ his mother

b) ☐ his girlfriend

c) ☐ his sister

d) ☐ Toni

	true	false	not given
5 Nick had never been in the flower shop before.	☐	☐	☐
6 Nick and Toni were alone in the flower shop.	☐	☐	☐
7 Toni knew that Martin was going to break off their relationship.	☐	☐	☐
8 Nick was in the same restaurant as Toni and Martin.	☐	☐	☐

2.2 Wortschatz: Roses and Mobiles

Toni sent an email to a friend to tell her what happened on Valentine's Day. The text below is part of her email.

Fill in suitable words, or tick the correct box.

1 Hi Sandy,
I must tell you ________________ my amazing Valentine's Day.

2 ... I was at work in the flower shop, this really good-looking guy came in.

a) ☐ While
b) ☐ During
c) ☐ Since
d) ☐ As

3 He wanted to buy ... roses.

a) ☐ any
b) ☐ some
c) ☐ few
d) ☐ much

4 He said they were for his sweetheart. I thought: "He's got a girlfriend already.

What a ________________."

5 After work I went to the big

________________ store in Harbour Street to buy a mobile phone.

6 ... things haven't been good between Martin and me, I wanted to give him a present.

a) ☐ If
b) ☐ In fact
c) ☐ Finally
d) ☐ Although

7 I went into the electronics department and – guess what! The guy working behind the

________________ was the good-looking guy from the flower shop!

8 He ... me his name was Nick.

a) ☐ said
b) ☐ described
c) ☐ told
d) ☐ explained

9 That evening Martin and I went out for dinner in a nice restaurant, and Martin said he wanted to break ... our relationship.

a) ☐ off
b) ☐ down
c) ☐ out
d) ☐ through

10 ________________ that moment the mobile phone, which was still in my bag, rang.

11 I was surprised because I didn't know that

anyone had the ________________.

12 I looked across the restaurant and Nick was

sitting ________________ another table.

13 There was a text message on the phone. It was ... Nick.

a) ☐ by
b) ☐ of
c) ☐ from
d) ☐ off

14 The message ________________ that his "sweetheart" was his sister.

2.3 Schreiben: Roses and Mobiles

Read the tasks carefully. Write complete sentences. Make sure you write about all the aspects presented in each task.

1 Your school website has a "Book Page", where students can write reviews of books, stories and poems which they have read. Write a review of the story *Roses and Mobiles* for the Book Page. Write about 80 words.
- Give a brief summary of the story.
- Say what you like or don't like about the story.
- Say if you would (or wouldn't) recommend the story to other students and why.

2 Look again at the short story *Roses and Mobiles*. Does it have a sad or a happy ending? Explain your answer by giving details from the story. Write at least 100 words.

3 Choose **one** of the following tasks
a) Choose one of the characters in the story and write a description of him or her. Imagine the details yourself. Describe the person's appearance, their character and interests. Invent some facts about their life. Write at least 120 words.

or:

b) What do you think happens after the story here ends? Write two more paragraphs for the story. Write at least 120 words.

TEST THREE

3.1 Leseverstehen: Different places, different lives

The two texts below are about a region in the far north of Canada called Nunavut.

Read the whole text and then the tasks. Read the text again and do the tasks.
In tasks 1–4 tick the correct answer. In tasks 5–8 decide if the statements are true, false or if there is no information in the text.

About Nunavut

Nunavut is the newest region of Canada. It became a separate region in 1999. It is also the largest region – over 2 million square kilometres. However, only 30,000 people live here (over 80 million live in Germany). The country is extremely cold and the winters are long and dark. The capital of the region is Iqaluit. Around 85 per cent of the people who live in Nunavut are the native people of this part of northern America. They are the Inuit. The name Nunavut means "Our Land" in Inuktitut, the language of the Inuit.

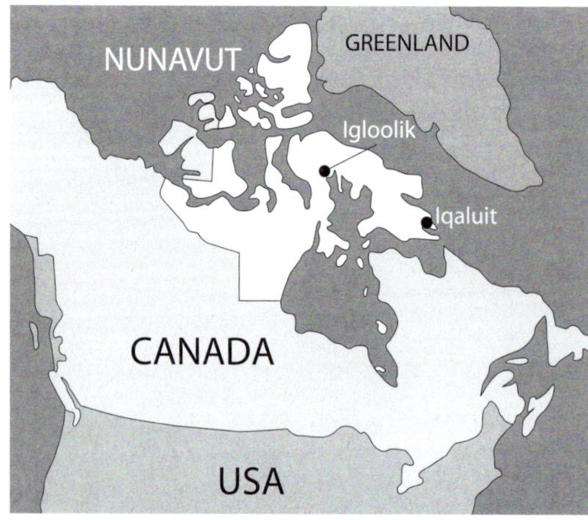

Benji Annanak, 16, from northern Canada goes to school by snowmobile.
The temperature where he lives is often -50 °C.

The part of Canada where I live is called Nunavut. It's in the far north of the country and up here it's COLD! The school I go to has 200 students, all kids from Igloolik (the town where I live), from the age of five to 18. Before they built the school ten years ago we all had to go to another town a hundred miles away and live there for nine months of the year, so it's good now that we can stay at home. The language we speak in school is English. We have more or less the same lessons as kids everywhere in Canada and when we're 18 we can get a High School Diploma – just like other young Canadians. We have the Internet and satellite TV, and there's a restaurant in Igloolik which sells burgers – you see, we're not so different from teenagers everywhere. At the same time, we're also a bit special! We can all speak Inuktitut – it's the language I use when I speak to my mom and dad – and in school we still learn the traditional things which Inuit people have always learned. We learn to fish, to hunt[1] and prepare animals for food, and to make clothes from the animals. Our sports in school are also traditional Inuit sports. My favourite is wrestling[2]. I'm the school champion :-). It's important for us that we don't forget our culture.

1 ***to hunt*** *jagen*
2 ***wrestling*** *Ringkampf*

1 Which of the following statements is correct?

a) ☐ Nunavut is the newest and coldest region in Canada.

b) ☐ Nunavut has more inhabitants than Germany.

c) ☐ Nunavut is the newest and largest region in Canada.

d) ☐ Winters in Nunavut are dark but short.

2 What is the most important town in Nunavut?

a) ☐ Igloolik

b) ☐ Iqaluit

c) ☐ Inuit

d) ☐ Inuktituk

3 How many of the people who live in Nunavut are native Americans?

a) ☐ a few

b) ☐ some

c) ☐ all

d) ☐ most

4 Why is learning about traditional things important for Inuit children?

a) ☐ So that they don't forget their culture.

b) ☐ So that they can get a High School Diploma.

c) ☐ So that they can be different from other teenagers.

d) ☐ So that they can survive the winter.

	true	false	not given
5 Benji's school is a hundred miles away from his home.	☐	☐	☐
6 Benji speaks one language at school and another at home.	☐	☐	☐
7 Benji's mom and dad can't speak English.	☐	☐	☐
8 Many things in Benji's life are the same as for other young Canadians.	☐	☐	☐

3.2 Wortschatz: Different places, different lives

Joe lives in Vancouver, Canada. He is going to give a presentation at school on Nunavut, a region in the far north of his country. Joe finds some information on the internet. The text below is part of his presentation.

Fill in suitable words, or tick the correct box.

Life in Nunavut

1 Nunavut is a region in Canada which is ... cold in the winter.

a) ☐ extreme
b) ☐ extremely
c) ☐ exaggerated
d) ☐ nicely

2 The temperature sometimes falls to minus

50 ________________.

3 The kids there often go to school ... snowmobile.

a) ☐ in
b) ☐ with
c) ☐ by
d) ☐ on

4 People have lived in Nunavut ... about 4000 years.

a) ☐ since
b) ☐ in
c) ☐ long
d) ☐ for

5 The name Nunavut ________________ "Our Land".

6 The native people in Nunavut teach their traditions to their children so that their

________________ does not get lost.

7 Many children speak their native

________________ at home with their parents.

8 ... they all speak English at school.

a) ☐ However,
b) ☐ Finally,
c) ☐ At least
d) ☐ Besides,

9 There are no roads or railways that

________________ Nunavut with other parts of Canada.

10 ... are not many tourists in Nunavut.

a) ☐ It
b) ☐ There
c) ☐ They
d) ☐ Their

11 But more and more people are ... this beautiful region.

a) ☐ inventing
b) ☐ coming
c) ☐ discovering
d) ☐ travelling

12 There are four wonderful national parks, and

you can ________________ many different kinds of sports, such as hiking and rock climbing.

13 ... the winters are long and dark, there are up to 24 hours of light per day from April to August.

a) ☐ Although
b) ☐ However
c) ☐ Because
d) ☐ Also

14 So spring and summer are the ________________ times to visit the region.

3.3 Schreiben: Different places, different lives

Read the tasks carefully. Write complete sentences. Make sure you write about all the aspects in each task.

1 Your school has started a project with Benji's school in Nunavut. You are sending emails to the school there and the Canadian pupils are writing emails to your class. Write an email. Compare your life, country and school with theirs. Write about 80 words.

2 Benji is travelling around Europe and today he is visiting your school. Write an interview with him. Imagine that he is in your class and people are asking him questions. You can use information from the text, but you should also think of other questions for Benji and imagine his answers. Write at least 100 words.

3 Choose **one** of the following tasks

a) Write an advertisement for Nunavut for a holiday brochure. Write at least 120 words about:
- the region
- the people and their traditions
- what you can do
- how you will travel
- the best time to visit

or:

b) Benji says: "It's important for us that we don't forget our culture." What does he mean by this? What sorts of things do people mean when they say "traditional culture" (language, sports, ...)? Do you agree that it is important that people remember their traditional culture? What things can be done to help people to remember their cultures (projects, exhibitions, ...)? Write at least 120 words.

A polar bear.

Nunavut's main airport in Iqaluit. All long-distance travel in Nunavut is by plane.

Vom Ausgangstext zum Zieltext

Test One

Robbie

The text below is a short story.

Read the text and do the tasks in 1.1 and 1.2.

Robbie

Dr Susan Calvin, the world's leading robot psychologist, sat back in her chair. "At the beginning ,the first robots were very primitive compared to today's," she began. "For one thing, they couldn't speak, and they were, well, a bit mechanical. Right from the start, they obeyed the laws of robotics, of course, and the first of those was that a robot may not injure a human being. But robots were new, and people were afraid of them. Take the case, for example, of Robbie ..."

"Ninety-eight, ninety-nine, one hundred. Coming!" Gloria opened her eyes and looked around the garden. Where was he? She couldn't see him in the bushes. "I bet he's gone into the house," she thought. "I've told him a million times that's not fair." Then she heard the clump-clump of Robbie's metal feet. Gloria shouted and laughed. It was so much fun playing with Robbie!

"Gloria! It's late. You have to come in now." It was Gloria's mother's voice. "I'm sorry, Mamma," said Gloria when she and Robbie reached the house. "I was playing with Robbie and I forgot the time." Mrs Weston's face was cold. "And I suppose you forgot the time too." She looked at Robbie. Robbie's head sank. "You can go now," she said to the robot. "And don't come back until I tell you."

George Weston, Gloria's father, was a kind and comfortable man. After a good lunch on Sunday, he liked to be alone to read the newspaper, and when the door opened and Mrs Weston came in, George pretended[1] not to notice. "George!" said Mrs Weston angrily. "Now, listen to me! It's about that robot. It isn't right that a metal thing like that looks after our daughter. These robots are new, and, well, something might happen." "Nonsense," said Mr Weston. "You know that Robbie could never harm Gloria. It's the first law of robotics, and they explained all that to us when we bought him." "Well, I don't like it," said Mrs Weston. "Robbie has to go."

George tried to argue with his wife for a week, but in the end, Robbie went. Gloria's heart was broken.

Two months later, Gloria had stopped crying, but she had also stopped smiling. She couldn't forget about Robbie. One evening Mrs Weston and her husband were sitting on the sofa. "Gloria needs something new and exciting to do," Mrs Weston said. "I suggest we go to New York for a month. We can rent a flat there, see the city–" "New York?" shouted Mr Weston.

"New York! Do you have any idea what New York is like in August? It's hot, it's ..." But Mr Weston loved his wife, and would try anything to make Gloria happy again. Arrangements were made, and at the beginning of August the family arrived in the city.

They saw everything there was to see. Gloria seemed interested in the new buildings and the museums. But every time they met a robot in the street she turned her head to look. It was clear that the vacation had not made her fully happy again. There were just two days left of their visit to the city. In the afternoon, Mr Weston disappeared mysteriously for a couple of hours. Later that evening, he said to his wife: "Look, I've been thinking. Gloria misses Robbie because she thinks he's a person. I've just been to see Fred Robertson from US Robot and Mechanical Men Inc.–" "Where we bought Robbie," interrupted Mrs Weston. "That's right," answered Mr Weston. "Well, he's arranged a tour of the factory for us tomorrow. Gloria can see how robots are made and that they're only machines."

The next morning, the family arrived at the factory. It was immense, and Mr Robertson guided them round the whole place. Finally, they went into a large room. "In here," he explained proudly, "there are no humans at all. Here, robots build other robots." Gloria looked round the room. In one corner, there were six robots, all working. Suddenly, her eyes lit up. It was Robbie! Robbie was one of the robots! "Robbie!" she called. "Robbie!" At that moment, two things happened. Gloria ran towards the robot and a large truck came fast across the floor – straight towards Gloria. The adults froze in horror. Only one thing moved. Robbie. With perfect precision, the robot ran towards the little girl, lifted her in its arms, and jumped from right in front of the truck.

Five minutes later, when she was a little calmer, Mrs Weston looked at her husband. "You arranged this, didn't you?" she said. "This trip to the factory where you knew Gloria would find Robbie. "Yes," admitted Mr Weston. "But that thing with the truck, I never arranged that." Mrs Weston looked at her daughter. She had never seen her so happy. "And you must admit," Mr Weston went on. "Robbie saved her life. You can't send him away again now." "Oh well, replied Mrs Weston. "I guess he can stay until he rusts[2]."

(Adapted and abridged from Robbie by Isaac Asimov)

1 ***to pretend (to do something)*** *to make it seem that something is true when it is not: He put on a hat and a uniform and pretended to be a policeman.*
2 ***to rust*** *metal 'rusts' – turns a brown colour – when it gets wet: A bicycle will rust if you leave it in the rain.*

1.1 Wortschatz: Robbie

1 When completed, the following expressions could all be used to write a review of a book or story. Match the halves of the expressions 1–9 and a–i. Write a–i in the boxes below.

1 The author of the story is	a) ... the topic / the idea of...
2 The story is set	b) in ... (e.g. the USA / the year 2003)
3 The main	c) in the story is this.
4 The book deals with	d) of this is ...
5 Very briefly, what happens	e) is one of the best/worst stories I've ever read.
6 One of the things I	f) ... (name of author)
7 An example	g) recommend this story.
8 In conclusion, I can say that this	h) characters in the story are ... (names)
9 I'd definitely (not)	i) like about the story is ...

1	2	3	4	5	6	7	8	9

2 Complete the diagram below about different types of fiction with at least ten words and expressions. Write in:
- some topics which each type of fiction deals with.
- some characters you could find in each type of fiction.

Love story

love

Murder story

detective

Science fiction story

Horror story

1.2 Schreiben: Robbie

1 First briefly describe who the main characters are in the story *Robbie*, then use the network diagram below to write about their relationships. Give examples from the text to illustrate your ideas. Write a total of at least 75 words for this question.

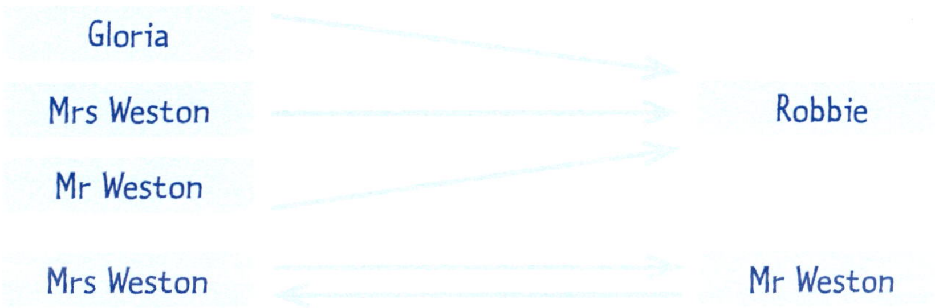

2 Read the two short texts below. How are they relevant to the story *Robbie*? Explain your answer with examples and quotations from the text. Write at least 100 words.

Ned Ludd was the leader of a movement in England in the early 1800s. "Luddites" were people who were against the new machines that were beginning to appear as a result of the Industrial Revolution – usually workers who were afraid that they would lose their jobs because of the new technology.

Authors can use stories in a number of different ways. They can tell a simple story which we read because we want to know what happens next. Or they can use a story to illustrate an idea. Often, in science fiction stories, they use a story set in the future to illustrate an idea about society in general.

3 Here you have a choice. Choose **one** of the following tasks:

a) Your school website has a "Book Page" where students can write reviews of books, stories and poems which they have read. Write a review of *Robbie* for the Book Page.
- Give a brief summary of the story.
- Say what you liked and disliked about it.
- Say if you would (or wouldn't) recommend the story to other students and why.

Write at least 100 words.

or:

b) Write about a story or a book that you have enjoyed.
- Give a brief summary of the story.
- Say what you liked and disliked about it.
- Say if you would (or wouldn't) recommend the story to other students and why.

Write at least 100 words.

TEST TWO

Aboriginal people in Australia

The pictures and the texts below deal with the history of the Aborigines in Australia.

Read the texts and do the tasks in 2.1 and 2.2.

An ancient[1] culture

Most scientists believe that the Aborigines came to Australia about 40,000 years ago and were the first people to inhabit[2] the continent. When the British arrived in Botany Bay in 1788, over 250 different clans existed with over 250 different languages. Their society was complex but well-ordered and stable. The British brought diseases with them that killed about 50 per cent of Australia's native population within a very short time.

The Aborigines soon lost control over their land, except in the remotest parts of the continent. Their culture was not respected and few Europeans took the trouble to learn about Aboriginal life and customs. The Queensland Act in 1897 meant that Aborigines often had to live on reserves under government administration[3]. They had few rights and their movements were limited. Aborigines had little chance of the same standards of education, health and employment as whites.

But gradually there were signs of change. Projects were started to improve employment and the health of Aborigine groups and to respect their languages and culture. Laws were passed to make Aborigines legally, socially and economically equal to whites. Equal pay for Aborigines was one of the first achievements. After 1971 they had the right to own land. But it took many more years before the Aborigines had equal rights in every way.

Aboriginal rock paintings

On 13th February, 2008 the Prime Minister, Kevin Rudd, made an official, public apology to members of the "stolen generations".

1 ***ancient*** *very, very old*
2 ***inhabit*** *live in*
3 ***administration*** *management*

A friend to the Aborigines

Daisy Bates was born in Ireland in 1859. At the age of 23 she emigrated to Australia. Daisy was a colourful character and it is thought that she left Ireland because of a scandal. In Australia she married several times – sometimes to more than one man at the same time (illegally, of course!).

During a visit to England, Daisy read a letter to *The Times* newspaper about how cruelly West Australian settlers treated the Aborigines of Australia. She wrote to *The Times* and offered to make a full investigation and report back to them. The offer was accepted and Daisy's career as a journalist began.

Daisy returned to Australia in 1899 and for the next 35 years she spent her life living with the Aborigines, studying their life, history, culture, beliefs and customs, and working for a better life for them. Most of the time she lived in a tent in an Aboriginal settlement[1]. Daisy always wore her old-fashioned clothes and veil[2], and right into her old age she always carried two pistols.

Daisy Bates died on 18 April 1951, aged 91.

1 ***Aboriginal settlement*** *area where the Aborigines live*
2 ***veil*** *a covering of fine material, worn by women to hide or protect the face*

2.1 Wortschatz: Aboriginal people in Australia

1 Find ten different nouns to fill in the diagram below.

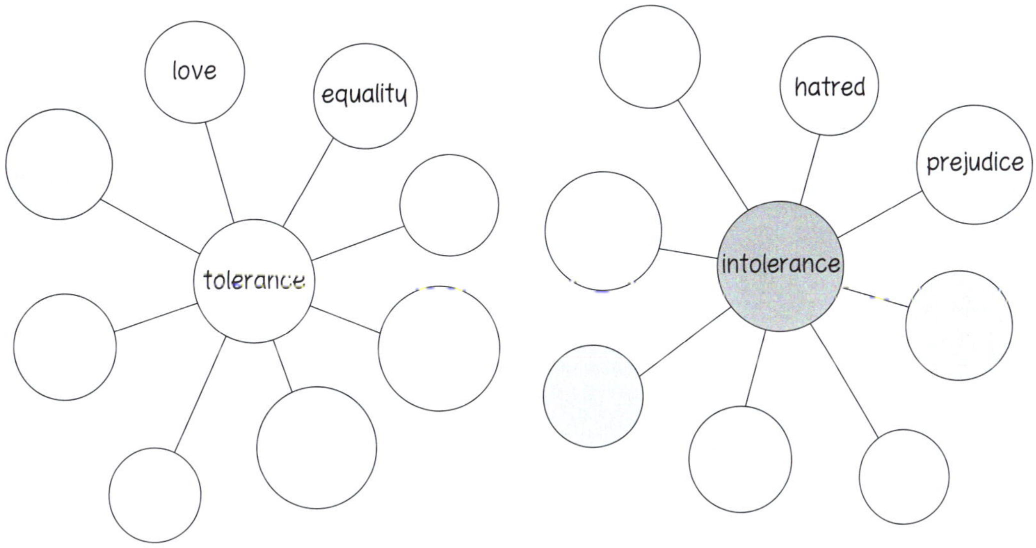

2 Complete the text below with the words and phrases for expressing opinions.

find it	firmly of the opinion	absolutely against
seems to me	point of view	far as I'm concerned

I am **1** ________________ discrimination in any form. Personally, I **2** ________________ disgusting that anyone should think they are better than anyone else just because of the colour of their skin, their language or their religion. As **3** ________________, people show whether they are good or bad by their behaviour and not by the way they look, or what they believe in. It **4** ________________ that people who look down on other people often feel inferior[1] themselves. I am **5** ________________ that we should do all we can to teach our children tolerance from a very early age. From my **6** ________________, parents, teachers and the media could do a lot more.

1 ***inferior*** *minderwertig*

2.2 Schreiben: Aboriginal people in Australia

1 Daisy Bates was fascinated by the Aboriginal people. In what ways can our lives be made richer through contact with other beliefs and cultures? What are the advantages of a multi-cultural society? Are there any disadvantages? Write at least 100 words.

2 Here you have a choice. Choose **one** of the following tasks:

a) While staying in Australia, you have the opportunity to talk to an older Aborigine person about his/her life and experiences during his/her childhood and youth. What questions would you ask him/her. Write about 100 words.

or:

b) Imagine you could meet Daisy Bates in her nineties. What questions would you ask her about her life and experience with the Aboriginal people. Write about 100 words.

3 What are your feelings about discrimination, such as that against the Aborigines? Do you know any other examples of discrimination in history either in your country, or in other countries? Can you describe some typical situations in which such discrimination can take place? Have you seen examples of it personally? Write at least 120 words.

Zentrale Prüfung

Englisch

Lösungsheft

Mittlerer Schulabschluss
Jahrgangsstufe 10 (B)
Nordrhein-Westfalen

Cornelsen

Vorwort zum Lösungsschlüssel

Die zentralen Prüfungen am Ende der Klasse 10 werden nach festgelegten kompetenzbezogenen Kriterien beurteilt und benotet. Die klare Vergabe von positiven Punkten für die verschiedenen Einzelaspekte steht im Vordergrund der Bewertung der Schülerleistung. Es werden Punkte vergeben für die Aufgaben zum Hör- und Leseverstehen, für die zum Wortschatz sowie für die zum Schreiben. In diesem Lösungsschlüssel werden zum einen die richtigen Lösungen für die Hör- und Leseaufgaben angegeben, Lösungsvorschläge für die Wortschatzaufgaben und Musterantworten und ausführliche Vorschläge für die kriterienbezogene Bewertung der Schreibaufgaben unterbreitet. Die Gewichtung der Bewertung bzw. Benotung der einzelnen Teilaufgaben sollte entsprechend den offiziellen Vorgaben erfolgen. Zur Bewältigung der in diesem Heft vorgeschlagenen Aufgaben sollte den Schülerinnen und Schülern soviel Zeit zur Verfügung gestellt werden, wie offiziell vorgesehen ist.

Aufgaben zur Überprüfung der Kompetenzen im Hör- und Leseverstehen
Da es relativ unproblematisch ist, Punkte für die richtigen Antworten zu den Aufgaben zum Hör- und Leseverstehen entsprechend der Vorgaben festzulegen, wird an dieser Stelle darauf verzichtet, konkrete Punktvorschläge anzugeben. In aller Regel kann ein Punkt für jede richtige Antwort bei den multiple-choice-Aufgaben oder den *true/false*-Aufgaben verteilt werden. Es gibt jedoch auch Aufgaben in diesem Teil, bei denen ein Satz ergänzt oder eine Antwort in einem zusammenhängenden Satz gegeben werden muss. Bei dieser Art der Aufgaben ist allerdings darauf zu achten, dass Rechtschreib- und ggf. Grammatikfehler, die in den Antworten zu diesen Teilaufgaben auftreten, nicht gewertet werden, es sei denn, es ist überhaupt nicht zu erkennen, ob die Schüler/innen die richtige inhaltliche Aussage getroffen haben.

Aufgaben zur Überprüfung des Wortschatzes
Die jeweilige Leistung in den Wortschatzaufgaben kann auf die in der Tabelle dargestellte Weise bewertet werden.

richtig geschriebene Einträge	> 6	6–9	10–12
Punkte	0	1	2

inhaltlich richtige Einträge	12/11	10/9	8/7	6/5	4/3	2/1
Punkte	6	5	4	3	2	1

Aufgaben zur Überprüfung der Schreibkompetenz
Den anspruchsvollsten Teil der Bewertung stellen die Aufgaben zur Überprüfung der Schreibkompetenz dar. Die Kriterienraster bei den Schreibaufgaben beziehen sich den offiziellen Vorgaben entsprechend auf die
- Inhaltliche Leistung
- Ausdrucksfähigkeit
- Sprachliche Richtigkeit (Orthographie, Grammatik, Wortschatz)

Zur Beurteilung der inhaltlichen Leistung der Texte der Schüler/innen werden entsprechende Vorschläge in Tabellenform den jeweiligen Musterantworten beigegeben. Es soll ausdrücklich darauf hingewiesen werden, dass die aufgelisteten Inhaltsaspekte und Punkte Vorschlagscharakter haben, die selbstverständlich verändert und individuellen Bedingungen angepasst werden können. Die sprachliche Leistung, und zwar das Ausdrucksvermögen und die sprachliche Korrektheit, können mit Hilfe dieses Rasters erfasst werden.

SPRACHLICHE LEISTUNG	PUNKTE	
AUSDRUCKSVERMÖGEN – DARSTELLUNGSLEISTUNG		
durchgängig verständlicher und leicht lesbarer Text	3	
vollständig formulierte Sätze	3	
Redemittel der Beschreibung und Begründung	3	
neben einfache Sätze treten manchmal komplexere Satzgefüge	3	
angemessener allgemeiner und thematischer Wortschatz	3	
SPRACHLICHE KORREKTHEIT		
Wortschatz und Rechtschreibung	3	
einfache Grammatik	3	

Teil I

Hörverstehen

Test one

1.1 My first day at work *page 8*

Hi, I'm Becky, and I'm going to tell you about my first day at work. As you can probably see from the picture of me it was, how can I put this, a *disaster*! First a bit about me. I left school at 18 and then I trained for a year as a secretary. I finished my course last summer. I applied for some jobs and I was lucky, I had an interview for one of them straight away, and I got a job in a nice company in the town where I live. The starting date for the job was the first of September. It was a Monday. When you start work, people – friends, family and so on – always have lots of advice for you. "Wear smart clothes!" "Don't expect to know everything straight away." "Smile." And so on. But the one piece of advice *everyone* gives you is: "Don't be late on your first day!"

Well, you know as well as I do, that when you get advice you think: "Oh yeah, I know that. Be late? Me? Never!" That's why, on Monday September the first, I set my alarm for six o'clock. I had to be at work at nine, and the bus journey from my house to the office was about twenty minutes. I don't know what happened with the alarm, but when I woke up it was twenty-five past eight. I couldn't believe it! I threw on some clothes, washed my face, drank a glass of water and ran out of the house at exactly eight thirty.

When I got out into the street, I looked for my bus. Had I missed it? No – there it was, just coming up the road. Great! I thought. Everything is OK! Did I say "OK"? I had to cross the road to catch the bus. Just as I got about half way across, a big, expensive car came round the corner. Really fast. I mean, really fast. I stopped in the road. The car stopped, just about a meter from me. I was really stressed out and angry and I, well, you know, shouted something at the driver that included the word "idiot" and told him a few other things that he probably didn't want to know about himself. He didn't say anything, just drove off.

I caught my bus and arrived at work at five to nine. By now I was calm and quite happy, looking forward to my first day. Actually, it was very exciting. My very first day at work! The woman who had interviewed me for the job, Ms Burns from the personnel department, met me at the reception desk. She showed me where I was going to work, introduced me to some colleagues, and then said: "Right, Becky. We'll just go and say 'hello' to the boss of your department, Mr Murray." She knocked on the door of an office, and we went in. There, behind the desk, was the man in the big car. I think I went very red. I was sure he was going to fire me. Actually, he was OK. He looked a bit embarrassed too. We shook hands and I left. We've never talked about that day, and now that I've been here for a couple of months everything is fine. But what a way to start a new job!

1 c)
2 the town where she lives.
3 a)
4 c)
5 drank a glass of water
6 b)
7 big, expensive car came round the corner really fast
8 idiot
9 b)
10 c)
11 She found that Mr Murray, her new boss, was the man in the big car. She thought he was going to fire her, but actually he was OK.
12 c)

1.2 Announcements and messages *page 10*

1

Ladies and gentlemen, we're sorry to announce that there are technical problems with this train, and it will be returning to New York Central station in a few minutes. There, passengers for Hartford and Boston should go to platform six, where another train will be waiting to take them to their destinations.

2

Hi, Mom. Chrissy here. Just to let you know that I'm staying over at Sandy's tonight. We're going to get a take-away and watch a DVD. Sandy's mom will take us to school tomorrow. Hope that's okay. Love you. Bye.

3

... and that was today's news. And now the weather forecast:
north-east England will be cold and windy, and there may be some snow on the hills. In the North

West it will be a rainy day, and the rain will move up into Scotland during the afternoon. The Midlands and Wales will be dry but cloudy. In southern England it will be a cool day but with a little sunshine.

4

G'day, shoppers. It's your lucky day. We have lots of great special offers for you.
Today – and only today – frozen food is 20 per cent cheaper! That includes frozen fruit, vegetables, pizzas and .... ice cream! What could be better than a cold ice-cream on a hot day like today? Go now to the frozen food section.

5

Good morning, ladies and gentlemen. Welcome aboard British Airways flight BA 978 to Berlin. Our flight time will be one hour fifty minutes. Our arrival time in Berlin will be 11.30 German time. German time is one hour ahead of British time. During the flight we will serve tea, coffee and sandwiches ...

1 false
2 true
3 false
4 false
5 true

1.3 Healthy eating *page 11*

Liza

Well, I think it's really easy to eat healthy food. Like, for example, you should try to eat five portions of fruit or vegetables every day, right? So, have some juice for breakfast, an apple or something at break and again at lunchtime, and then, if you have some vegetables and fruit in the evening, that's five portions. I always eat like that.

Nadja

Doctors and the government are always saying that we should eat more healthy food. Well, I try, but one reason why it's hard is all the advertising on TV. I mean, you can't watch TV without adverts for sweets and fast food every few minutes. And that makes me want to eat those things! Why don't they advertise apples and carrots and things like that? There should be more adverts for healthy things, not just for fast food.

Daniel

I know it's a good idea to eat lots of vegetables and fruit and things, but they're just boring. I sometimes try to eat healthy stuff, because I know it's important, but burgers and chips just taste nicer. Often my mum's too busy to cook, so she gives me some money to buy my lunch, and, well, it's just quicker and cheaper to buy fast food.

Adam

I think they should have clearer labels on food so that we can see quickly what's healthy and what's unhealthy. For example, a kind of traffic-lights system; you know, a green light for healthy food, a yellow light for foods where you have to be a bit careful, and a red light for things you should eat as little as possible, like things with a lot of fat or salt. Don't you think that's a good idea?

Ashley

I would never, never, never buy fast food because I love cooking! It isn't difficult to make easy, healthy dishes. Everyone can do it. There are some great TV cooks like Jamie Oliver in England and Tim Mälzer in Germany. I love to watch their shows. I always get great ideas from them, and then I try new things on my family. So far, everyone has survived my experiments!

Liza	B
Nadja	D
Daniel	C
Adam	F
Ashley	A

Test two

2.1 My plans for the future *page 12*

Matt

Hi. I'm Matt Nilsson. I'm sixteen years old and I'm from the USA. I live in Miami, Florida, and this year I'm in the tenth grade in high school. My favorite subjects in school are math and history.
I have quite a lot of interests and hobbies. I like sports of all kinds, and in high school I play baseball and football. I also like music very much and I play the electric guitar in a band with some friends. When I'm not playing a sport or playing with the band, I like surfing the internet.

I plan to stay in high school until I'm 18. After that, I'd like to go to college, which is usually for four years here in the States. I'd like to study business at college because I'd like a job in business. I'm not sure what I want to do exactly, but perhaps marketing would be interesting. I like meeting people, and in marketing you're with people all the time. I think that would be good.

Zoe
G'day. I'm Zoe Taylor and I live in Sydney, Australia. I'm 17 years old and at present I'm a student in year 11 at an Australian high school. I really like my school and I enjoy most subjects, but my favourites are definitely art and science subjects such as physics and chemistry.

Sydney is a city near the sea, so my hobbies include swimming and playing volleyball on the beach. Because I love art at school, I also like photography and painting. Like all teenagers, I guess, I also listen to music and go out with my friends.

My plan is to stay at school for one more year until I'm 18. Then I'd like to go to university, probably in Sydney where I live.

I have known since I was a kid what I want to do as a career. I want to be an architect. I am really interested in buildings. As an architect you work not only in an office but also outside a lot. I'm a very active person, so I think that would be good for me.

1 b)
2 a)
3 a)
4 c)
5 b)
6 c)
7 a)
8 b)

2.2 My year abroad *page 13*

Hello! My name is Jürgen and I am a seventeen year-old boy from Germany staying in New Zealand for a year. I have been here for four months now, and I've really enjoyed my time so far.

At Geraldine High School, I'm living with a host family. My family is awesome! They are just so nice. They live about five minutes from the school and I walk to school each day with my host brother, Mike.

The weather in New Zealand is a bit different from the weather in Germany. When I first arrived I came straight from the German summer into a New Zealand winter and it was really cold. We had snow nearly every day. Now it's summer and we have some warm, sunny days.

We do lots of outdoor sporting activities here at the school. In the winter, I really enjoyed the skiing. Now we're doing rock climbing, kayaking, and rafting. You can do these things in Germany, of course, but here the mountains and everything are so close, so the activities are so easy to do. I like sports very much, so these kinds of activities are great for me.

School is more relaxed here than in Germany, I think. When I arrived, the school advised me to do fewer subjects than at home so I can make full use of my time in New Zealand. In Germany, I was doing 13 subjects and now here I am doing only 6 subjects. Another difference is that the school here organises more social activities for the students. There are dances, music evenings, fashion shows and lots of other things, so I meet students in the evenings as well as during the day.

The International Programme is very good too. There are eight international students at Geraldine this year, including me. They are from all over the world – Japan, Belgium, Denmark, Hong Kong and other countries. I'm the only one from Germany. Two of the Geraldine High School teachers take special care of us and help us organise things. We have had some nice trips with them to cities like Christchurch and Dunedin and to Wellington on North Island. We've also been to Lake Tekapo, which is absolutely beautiful.

Geraldine itself is a quiet little town with not many parties on the weekend. The next biggest town where you can go shopping is Timaru, about 30 minutes away. Many students live on farms near Geraldine.

My English has really improved, which of course I'm happy about. We have special English lessons in school, and I speak English all the time with my host family. But improving my English wasn't my main reason for coming here. I came for the experience of getting to know another country and culture, living with another family, and meeting new people. I have eight more months ahead of me, and a summer holiday, so I'm looking forward to the rest of my year here.

1 true
2 false
3 false
4 true
5 false
6 true
7 true
8 false
9 false
10 false

Christopher I think the most important thing about writing is planning. I spent a long time thinking and planning before I began the trilogy. I even made a map of Dragonland so I knew exactly where all the places were. If you don't have a good plan, you'll never write a good story. After that, writing the text isn't so hard. But you need to know exactly where you're going with the story first.

Interviewer Two of your books are out, then, Christopher and the third will be out next year. Can you tell us what will happen in the third book? Will it have a happy ending?

Christopher I'm afraid you'll have to buy the book and read it when it appears.

Interview So you won't tell us how the trilogy ends?

Christopher Sorry, no way.

Interviewer OK. Christopher, thanks very much indeed for this interview.

Christopher You're welcome.

1 true
2 true
3 false
4 false
5 false
6 true
7 false
8 true
9 true
10 true

3.3 Coming to America *page 18*

Larry Janaczek

My name is Larry Janaczek. I was six when I came to America with my grandparents and parents in 1932. We arrived in New York in the early morning, and went straight to the Immigration Building on Ellis Island. I can still remember it, although I was very young at the time. The place was chaos – about 3,000 people a day were passing through there at that time. They asked us lots of questions: What's your name? Where are you from? Have you got somewhere to live? Can you read? We had to see a doctor, who looked into our eyes and mouths. And all the time we thought: Will it be OK? Will they let us in? If you had a bad disease, you see, they put you back on the boat and sent you home. Then at last we were through, and they gave us a meal of soup, bread and milk. And I looked at the Immigration Hall. It was so big and so grand, and I thought: this is going to be good. America is going to be good!

Maria Contonelli

I'm Maria Contonelli. I was just a baby when my family came to America from Italy in 1923. There was me, my six brothers and sisters, my parents and my grandmother. We lived in one of the tenement buildings on the East Side. We kids all slept in one room with my grandmother, and mom and dad had the other room. The place was filthy and there was only one toilet for everyone on our floor. In Italy, we had been poor but there, my grandmother always said, people were clean. And there the sun shone every day. Grandma used to say to my parents: "This is America? Why did you bring me to America?" But I was only a baby so I remembered nothing of the country where I was born.

Miriam Hassan

Hi. I'm Miriam Hassan. I'm 15 years old and I moved from Kenya to the United States three years ago. We came here because my parents wanted a better life for us all.

When we arrived here, everything was new and different. We have cities in Kenya, but Atlanta is just so big! In Kenya, we were always near to the countryside, and there were lots of animals and trees and flowers. I sometimes still miss the countryside and the animals in Kenya.

I was a bit lonely when I first came, but everyone at my school was friendly and asked a lot of questions about my country. Fortunately, we speak English in Kenya so the language wasn't a big problem.

I think my life here is better. My school is great and there are so many things I can do that I couldn't do in Kenya. My mom and dad have good jobs, and we all know that America is the right place for us.

Fali Khan

My name is Fali Khan. Life in my home country, Pakistan, was good because all my cousins and friends lived nearby and we had a lot of fun together. But our family was very big, and it was hard for my dad, who was the only one who had a job. When I was fifteen, my parents decided to come to America. We had to leave my eldest sister and brother in Pakistan because they were over 21 and couldn't come with us. It was very sad. It was a long trip – two days in the airplane.

Now my father and my brothers all have good jobs. My sister and I study in high school. Everyone works hard and we hope to buy our own house one day. Everything is good. The only problem is that my mom really misses my eldest brother and sister. She always thinks about them. I hope they come here one day, then my mom will be happy.

Larry	C, F
Maria	B, G
Miriam	A, D
Fali	E, H

Test four

4.1 Horrible jobs *page 19*

Peter The worst job I can imagine is one where I have to do the same thing every day – say, like working in a factory, a job with a lot of routine, where you'd get really bored, and where you don't earn much money, and you've got no future. Or an office job, where you only work with papers and documents, and you have eight hours a day to kill. I think I'd go mad!

Jill Oh, Peter, there are jobs that are a lot worse than that. Think about dangerous jobs, or dirty jobs. For example, I read somewhere that the most dangerous job in America is a woodcutter. The death rate is thirty times higher than in a typical workplace. The next most dangerous is a fisherman. The third most dangerous is a roofer – you know, the people who repair your roof.

Adil I agree with Jill. Danger is much worse than boredom. But I imagine that there are some jobs that are just horrible to do. I wonder, for example, who makes his or her living by killing all the animals we eat, you know, all the chickens for our soup, and the cows for our burgers?

Jill Ugh, Adil, stop! I can't stand it! I'm glad I'm a vegetarian.

Adil Or a dirty job such as working in a hospital laundry.

Peter Oh, yeah. I once saw a programme called 'Dirty Jobs' on the Discovery Channel. This guy called Mike Rowe did the dirtiest jobs you can imagine, to show us how some people spend their working day. For example, you know that blue cheese dip you get with your chicken wings? Well, somebody has to make it, and there are factories that produce it. The smell is horrible, and people actually work there. Mike Rowe interviewed some of them, and funnily enough, they looked quite happy!

Jill What's the worst job you've ever had, Adil?

Adil I once worked in a restaurant kitchen as a dishwasher. We had to put the food that was left on the plates into an enormous bin. By the end of the day the bin was full of a mixture of all kinds of stuff. It was disgusting. Sometimes I cut myself on the knives and forks, and if we broke anything, we had to pay for it. It was a horrible job – and the pay was really low.

Peter The worst job I ever had was as a nightwatchman. It was very boring and I found it hard to stay awake with no-one to talk to and nothing much to do. The hours were endless. I also got nervous whenever I heard an unusual noise. My imagination went wild! What about you, Jill? What's the worst job you've ever done?

Jill Well, I've never had a dangerous or dirty job, but once, when I was a student, I worked for a telephone marketing company, and it was just SO boring. It was like dial, dial, dial, ring, ring, ring, "Good morning, this is ..." – and they'd hang up on you! Frustrating! And I had to do that at least a hundred times a day.

Adil Okay, so we all agree that horrible jobs are dangerous, dirty and/or boring. So what's your ideal job?

Peter I like my job now, but I'd like to travel more and ...

1 a)
2 fisherman, roofer
3 b)
4 b)
5 hospital laundry
6 a)
7 c)
8 b)
9 no-one to talk to, nothing much to do
10 c)

4.2 Brothers and sisters *page 21*

Chloe Tansu, James. Tell us about your brothers and sisters.

Tansu Well, I have two brothers, both of them are older than me.

Chloe I'd love to have an older brother.

Tansu Well, it has its disadvantages. My brothers sort of feel responsible for me, and sometimes that gets in the way of things I want to do!

Chloe I only have a sister and she's younger than me. When she was born, I was really jealous of her. She had lovely blonde hair. One day – I don't know where my mum was – I took a pair

Lucy Oh, yeah. I've had dreams like that, too. I wonder where nightmares come from.
Jake Oh, I read something about that once. It's because your brain doesn't switch off when you are asleep. It keeps working. There are quite a few reasons for nightmares. They are often the brain's way of dealing with stress. It's completely normal.
Ryan Well, I'm glad I'm normal.
Jake Well, there are always exceptions, of course!

1 false
2 true
3 false
4 false
5 true
6 false
7 true
8 false
9 false
10 false

5.3 Friendship *page 26*

Finlay
Friendship? Well, my idea of friendship is that it's all about give and take. Who decides which film to watch, or where to go at the weekend? Sometimes it can be you and sometimes your friend. Nobody should always get their own way.

Sophie
What's a good friend? I think a good friend is somebody who is always there for you. If he or she phones and needs you, ten minutes later you should be there to help. You should never have anything more important to do if your friend needs to talk.

Conor
I think a real friend will tell you what he or she really thinks when you ask for an opinion. They don't just tell you what you want to hear. That's what a friend is for. Sometimes it hurts, but it's better in the end.

Harry
If your friend has something you haven't got – more money, a new bike, a laptop – you shouldn't think: "That's not fair" or "Why him and not me?" You should be happy for him or her.

Isabelle
If you tell your friend: "I'll see you on Saturday," then you must be there on Saturday. If you forget, even if you say you're sorry, it will hurt your friend and sooner or later the friendship will break up.

Finlay	C
Sophie	A
Conor	F
Harry	B
Isabelle	D

LESEVERSTEHEN

TEST ONE

1.1 Who speaks English *page 27*

1 d)
2 b)
3 Britain, (the) USA, Australia, New Zealand
4 c)
5 They are learning it/English at school.
6 b)
7 (much) pop culture, (the) internet, business
8 b)

1.2 Looking for a job *page 29*

0 G 1 E 2 B 3 C 4 D 5 F

TEST TWO

2.1 Are you addicted to the internet? *page 31*

1 d)
2 c)
3 a)
4 c)
5 Anton
6 a) Emily
b) She also loves reading, going shopping with friends, etc.
7 a) Sophie
b) She chats to all her English friends online.
8 You can chat to friends. You can get help with homework. You can send and receive emails. (You can improve your English. You can play games.)

2.2 Holiday activities *page 33*

0 C 1 B 2 D 3 A 4 E 5 G

TEST THREE

3.1 Buy Nothing Day *page 35*

1 c)
2 b)
3 false
The text says one million people all over the world took part in BND last year.
4 true
The text says that BND was first started by Ted Dave back in 1992.
5 a)
6 d)
7 20: 20% of the world's population consumes 86% of the world's natural resources.
65: BND now takes place in around 65 countries all over the world.
1995: Adbusters took up Ted Dave's idea of BND in 1995.
33: We spend $33 billion per year worldwide on make-up and perfume.
1.3: For $1.3 billion all children in the Third World could be immunised.

3.2 Magazines *page 37*

0 B 1 F 2 D 3 E 4 G 5 C

TEST FOUR

4.1 Barack Obama *page 39*

1 **1**B, **2**E, **3**C, **4**F, **5**A
2 c)
3 Hawaii, Indonesia (Jakarta), New York, Chicago
4 c)
5 b)
6 d)
7 a)
8 lawyer, teacher, director of a community project, senator, (President of the USA)
9 American, Kenyan, Indonesian
10 4: Barack Obama made history on November 4th 2008 (when he won the presidential election in the USA).
20: Obama was ten when he returned to Hawaii (to live with his grandparents).
1982: In 1982 Obama's father died in a car accident.
12: Obama taught law at the University of Chicago Law School for twelve years.
44: Obama is the 44th President of the USA.

4.2 Books *page 42*

0 C 1 E 2 F 3 G 4 D 5 A

TEST FIVE

5.1 The power of nature *page 44*

1 waterfalls, floods, tidal waves
2 c)
3 1000 (one thousand)
4 a)
5 It falls/they fall out of the sky./It is/they are brought by the wind.
6 It is a huge, endless wave.
7 d)
8 **Jack:** Black Sun
Jill: The fastest wind
Oliver: The biggest hailstorms
Sandy: It's raining frogs
Jim: The longest wave on earth

5.2 A place to live *page 46*

0 D 1 A 2 G 3 B 4 E 5 F

weekends, he swims and surfs in the sea. He is about 20 years old. He has a lot of good friends and a younger sister, who also lives in Sydney with their parents. Nick has his own flat in the city centre. He works in the electronics department of a Sydney department store, and because he is a friendly person and interested in modern technology and gadgets, he is very good at his job. I think I would like Nick – if he existed! (127 words)

Inhaltliche Bewertung:

ASPEKT	PUNKTE	
Nick Bensley from Australia	1	
Tall, good-looking	1	
Brown hair, blue eyes	1	
Athletic, Wears nice clothes	1	
Likes sports, especially water sports	1	
Swims and surfs after work or at weekends	1	
About 20 years old	1	
Has a sister who lives with parents in Sydney	1	
Has lots of friends	1	
Lives in his own flat in the centre of Sydney	1	
Works in the electronics department of a Sydney department store	1	
Good at his job	1	
... because he is friendly and interested in technology and gadgets	2	
Ending: I would like/dislike Nick because ...	2	
GESAMTLEISTUNG	**16**	

3 b) *(Lösungsvorschlag)*
When Nick got Toni's message on his mobile, he smiled. He looked very happy. Toni went back to her table and sat down. She looked at Martin. He looked worried. "I'm sorry about our relationship, Toni," he said. "I hope you understand." "It's OK," said Toni. I understand, but I'd like to go now." "Of course," said Martin.

Toni stood up and left the restaurant. Outside she waited, and a few moments later, Nick came out. "What happened with your fiancé?" he asked Toni. "It's all over," she said. "Martin has broken off the relationship." Nick smiled again. Toni smiled, too. "This is the best Valentine's Day of my life," she said. Nick took her hand and they walked through the city to the sea. It was a beautiful, warm night and the moon was shining. The two kissed. (139 words)

Inhaltliche Bewertung:

ASPEKT	PUNKTE	
Introduction	1	
Nick was happy about the text message	1	
Martin said he was sorry about the relationship	1	
Toni said she understood	1	
Toni left the restaurant	1	
She waited outside for Nick	1	
Nick came out of the restaurant	1	
Toni told him it was over with Martin	1	
Best Valentine's Day of Toni's life	1	
Walked together to the sea	1	
Romantic atmosphere	1	
Ending: The two kissed	1	
GESAMTLEISTUNG	**12**	

Test Three

3.1 Leseverstehen: Different places, different lives *page 56*

1 c)
2 b)
3 d)
4 a)
5 false
6 true
7 no information in the text
8 true

3.2 Wortschatz: Different places, different lives *page 58*

1 b)
2 degrees
3 c)
4 d)
5 means
6 culture
7 language
8 a)
9 connect

10 b)
11 c)
12 do
13 a)
14 best

3.3 Schreiben: Different places, different lives *page 59*

1 *(Lösungsvorschlag)*

I think there's a big contrast between your school in Igloolik and my school here in Germany. One of the biggest differences is the size. There are only 200 students at your school – there are 2000 at mine!

At your school you also learn about Inuit traditions like hunting and fishing. We don't learn things like that here.

I go to school by bike everyday and you go by snowmobile. I think that would be more fun!

(78 words)

Inhaltliche Bewertung:

ASPEKT	PUNKTE	
Big contrast between schools in Igloolik and Germany	**2**	
Very big difference in size, 200:2000	**2**	
Learn traditional Inuit things like hunting and fishing	**2**	
Nothing like that in schools in Germany	**2**	
Go to school by bike in Germany, by snowmobile in Nunavut	**2**	
Ending/opinion	**2**	
GESAMTLEISTUNG	**12**	

2 *(Lösungsvorschlag)*

Class What do you do with your friends in Nunavut in your free time?

Benji We sometimes watch TV or movies on the internet. We go fishing. We hang out in the burger restaurant, and sometimes we have snowmobile races.

Class What sports do you like?

Benji I like traditional Inuit sports like wrestling.

Class Do you want to live in Nunavut when you finish high school?

Benji I'm not sure. Perhaps I could get a better job in another part of Canada. I could work there for a year or two, but I think Nunavut is really my home.

Class What do you think of Europe?

Benji It's very crowded and very warm!

(106 words)

Inhaltliche Bewertung:

ASPEKT	PUNKTE	
Free time?	**1**	
Watch TV, movies in the Internet, fishing, burger restaurant, snowmobile races	**5**	
Sports?	**1**	
Inuit sports like wrestling	**2**	
Stay in Nunavut after high school?	**1**	
Not sure -perhaps better job in another part of Canada	**2**	
Work there for a year or two but Nunavut is home	**2**	
Opinion of Europe?	**1**	
Crowded and warm	**2**	
GESAMTLEISTUNG	**17**	

3 a) *(Lösungsvorschlag)*

Visit Nunavut for a new experience!

Nunavut is the newest and largest region of Canada. It is a beautiful region in the far north of the country, and it gets very cold in winter.

Only 30,000 people live there. About 85 per cent of them are Inuit, the native people of the region. They speak their own language and teach their children their old traditions, such as fishing, hunting and preparing animals for food. If you go to Nunavut, you can visit the national parks (there are four), or do sports such as hiking and rock climbing. All long-distance travel is by air, and the region is not connected by road or rail to other parts of Canada. The best time to visit is in spring or summer, when the days are long and there are up to 24-hours of light. (141 words)

Inhaltliche Bewertung:

ASPEKT	PUNKTE	
Newest and largest region in the north of Canada	**2**	
Beautiful region but very cold in winter	**2**	
About 30,000 people live there, 85 percent Inuit	**2**	
Own language	**1**	
Teach children traditions such as fishing, hunting and preparing animals for food	**3**	
Four national parks	**1**	

NOTES

NOTES